THE ZEN LIFE

Zen Life

photographs by Sosei Kuzunishi
text by Koji Sato

translated by Ryojun Victoria

WEATHERHILL/TANKOSHA
New York, Tokyo, Kyoto

This book was originally published in Japanese
by Tankosha under the title *Zen no Seikatsu*.

First English Edition, 1972

Jointly published by John Weatherhill, Inc., 149 Madison Avenue,
New York, N.Y. 10016, with editorial offices at 7-6-13 Roppongi,
Minato-ku, Tokyo 106, and Tankosha, Kyoto. Copyright © 1966,
1972, by Tankosha; all rights reserved. Printed in Japan.

LCC Card No. 79-185602   ISBN 0-8348-1508-7

Contents

THE ZEN LIFE

Part I: A PHOTO-ESSAY

1. A window of the Zendo (Hall for the Practice of Zazen). The shape is derived from the head of a flame.

2. The Sammon (lit., Mountain Gate) of Empuku-ji monastery. The Sammon receives its name from the fact that in China Zen monasteries were generally situated on the sides or tops of mountains. In Japan the Sammon has retained its name despite the fact that many Zen monasteries are located on level land, near or within cities.

3. A statue of one of the two guardian kings (Nio) of Em-puku-ji.

4. The path from the Sammon to the priests' quarters (*kuri*).

5. The tile roof of the Zendo.

6. The entrance to the priests' quarters. The Chinese characters on the pillar read, "It is forbidden to leave your straw sandals in a disorderly manner." The wooden clappers hanging on the wall are used to inform the monks of various monastic activities.

7. The roof of the Hondo (Main Hall). It is in this hall that a statue of the historical Buddha, Shakyamuni, is enshrined, hence it is also known as the Buddha Hall. Zen monks recite the Buddhist sutras (scriptures) here daily and perform various religious services on behalf of lay believers.

Gaining Entrance

8. A young novice priest (*unsui*) asks permission to enter into training at the monastery. The monk official of the monastery, however, bluntly refuses his request.

9. Visitors ring the bell in the foreground to notify monastery officials of their arrival. Behind it stands a single-panel screen with an abstract calligraphic design.

10. The novice monk maintains this same posture all day as a sign of his fervent desire to enter into training at the monastery.

◁ 11 (opposite page). After approximately three days of waiting the novice monk is given permission to enter the monastery temporarily. Before entering, however, he must first remove his straw sandals.

12. Washing one's feet thoroughly in order not to soil the tatami (straw mats) is an important part of Zen training.

13. Tying up one's straw sandals and *tabi* (white cotton socks) must also not be overlooked.

14. A wooden sounding board (*han*) which is struck to announce various daily activities in the monastery. The inscription on it reads, "No one knows when death will occur; it may be much sooner than one expects. Therefore we should practice Buddhism without wasting even a moment of time in order that we may discover the true meaning of life."

15. After the novice monk is given temporary permission to enter the monastery he is placed in a special room (*tankaryo*). Here his determination to enter monastic life is further tested for a period lasting between three to five days, the length of time depending on the earnestness with which he practices zazen. It is after clearing this second hurdle that the young novice is first allowed to join the community of monks and practice zazen in the Zendo.

16. The hallway leading from the priests' quarters to the Hondo. The polished look of the floor comes not from the use of wax but rather from the daily rubbing it receives with a damp cloth.

17. The two monastery bulletin boards. The upper one lists the major religious observances at the monastery during the year. The lower one lists the names of the monks, nuns, and laymen who are presently training in the monastery.

18. A stone pagoda located in the monastery garden. In Japan these pagodas are more often made of wood and are erected to enshrine the sacred relics of the historical Buddha or other religious objects.

19. The well that formerly supplied the monastery with water.

20. Firewood to be used for cooking, heating water for bathing, etc., is stacked near the Sammon.

Starting the Day

21. The sounding board is struck vigorously to awaken the monastery's inhabitants. The monks usually rise at 3:30 A.M. in summer and 4:00 A.M. in winter.

23. In washing the hands or face care must be taken ▷
so that not even a drop of water is wasted.

22. Teeth are brushed in the traditional manner, using only a finger and a little salt.

24. While ringing a hand bell a monk recites special morning sutras before Idaten, one of the guardian deities of the monastery.

Sutra Recitation

25. Sutras are recited in the Hondo both in the early morning and in the evening. The baton that the monk is holding is used to strike an inverted bell-shaped gong, indicating various stages in sutra recitation.

26. The instrument in the foreground is a *mokugyo* (literally, wooden fish). As it is hollow on the inside it produces a mellow tone when struck, providing the rhythm for sutra recitation.

Eating Meals

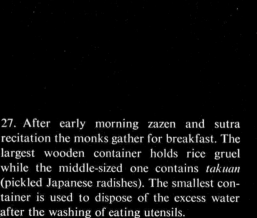

27. After early morning zazen and sutra recitation the monks gather for breakfast. The largest wooden container holds rice gruel while the middle-sized one contains *takuan* (pickled Japanese radishes). The smallest container is used to dispose of the excess water after the washing of eating utensils.

◁ 28. A monk places his eating bowls on the table and then waits with folded hands to be served.

29. The afternoon and evening meals consist of wheat mixed with rice, vegetable soup, and *takuan*. In the evening an additional bowl of boiled vegetables is generally added.

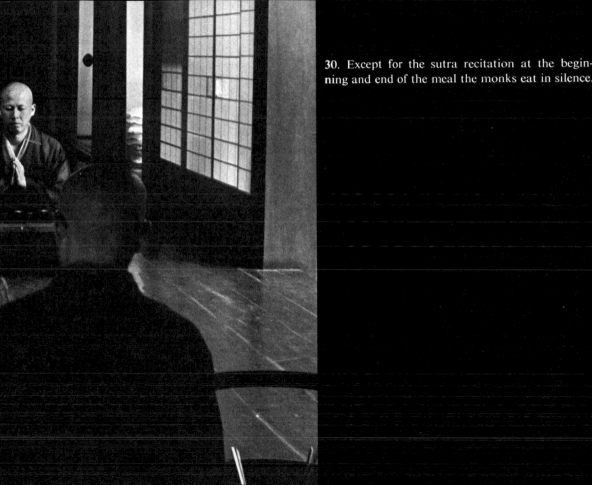

30. Except for the sutra recitation at the beginning and end of the meal the monks eat in silence.

◁ 31. A few grains of rice are collected from each monk to be used as an offering to the "hungry spirits" (*gakki*); i.e., to the spirits of those deceased persons who have not yet realized Buddhahood and are thought to be suffering from hunger as one of the torments of hell.

32. In actuality the rice collected in the wooden scoop is placed outside the monastery kitchen to be eaten by birds.

◁ 33. After a monk washes his bowls he empties the excess water noiselessly into this wooden bucket. Each monk must take care that not even one grain of rice that may have been clinging to his bowl is heedlessly disposed of.

34. The basic hand position prescribed for monks when they are walking is known as *shashu* (forked hands).

35. A monk strikes the *kansho* (calling bell) to notify the Zen master (roshi) that he wishes to have a private interview with him. During this interview the monk may ask questions concerning problems he is encountering in his practice of zazen, or he may present his "answer" to the *koan* (Zen riddle) the roshi had previously assigned him as the focal point for his zazen.

36. The monks tensely wait their turn to be interviewed by the master. Should their "answer" to the *koan* be mistaken or should they betray a lack of earnestness during the interview it is not unusual for them to be severely scolded or even struck by the roshi.

37. When monks meet in the monastery corridors they bow in reverence to each other with the palms of their hands pressed together in *gassho*.

38. Directly in front of the roshi's room the monk once more strikes a metal sounding instrument (*umpan*) before entering. Simply by listening to the way in which the *umpan* is struck the roshi is able to tell the degree of enlightenment of the monk.

39. Zen training is concerned with not only zazen but also all daily actions, even to the arrangement of one's straw sandals.

40. Zen lectures (*teisho*) consist of the roshi's discourses on Buddhist sutras and traditional Zen anecdotes. No attempt is made to give an intellectual explanation of the material, but rather the roshi makes "living comments" based on his own experience.

The Tea Ceremony

41. Striking wooden clappers together, a monk announces the commencement of the tea ceremony.

42. The roshi takes his place together with the other monks, and they all express their gratitude for the tea they are about to receive by bowing deeply.

43. The performance of the tea ceremony in a Zen monastery also serves as a method of keeping check on the monks' whereabouts.

44. Just as at mealtime, silence is maintained as the tea is poured and received. The very elaborate Japanese tea ceremony for laymen which developed in medieval times and is still popular in modern Japan finds its origin in this simple yet austere Zen practice.

Mendicancy

-worn Japanese-style sandals (*waraji*) made
straw are hung to dry until used again.

46. The wicker hats (*ajirogasa*) worn by the monks serve not only to protect their shaven heads from the sun's rays but also as umbrellas in case it rains.

47. Wearing *waraji* and holding their ▷ wicker hats in their hands the monks leave the monastery to begin practicing religious mendicancy (*takuhatsu*). The monks will not put on their wicker hats until after they have left the monastery grounds.

48. On the way to the nearby villages the monks walk in single file. Once again the rule of silence prevails.

49. The bamboo groves and ricefields surrounding the monastery form an extremely picturesque background as the monks begin their journey.

50. All the donations the monks collect during mendicancy are placed in cloth bags that are worn suspended by a strap around their necks. The Chinese characters on the bag read: "Empuku-ji Monastery."

51. In Zen shabby robes are nothing to be proud of; yet, even less are they something to be ashamed of. The true spirit of mendicancy may be said to find its fullest expression in this very fact.

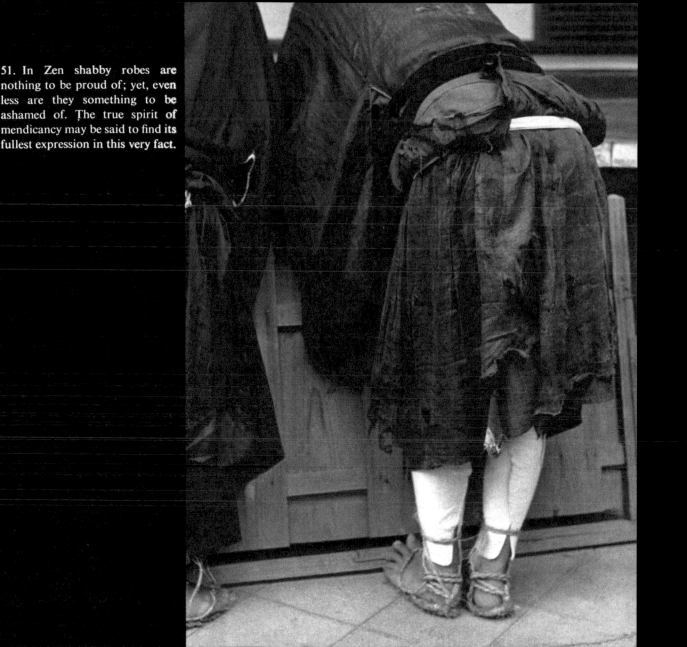

52. Upon arriving in a nearby village the monks walk from house to house reciting sutras on the way.

53. Sometimes the donations consist ▷ of rice, sometimes of money. Whatever each individual monk receives, however, becomes the property of the whole community of monks, to be used for their common benefit.

54. When a monk receives a donation he will recite a short sutra expressing his desire that all sentient beings may achieve Buddhahood, but he does not directly express any gratitude to the donor himself.

55 (left). During mendicancy the opportunity to relax at a wayside temple is a welcome break. But before relaxing the monks first show their appreciation by reciting a sutra in front of the Hondo.

56 (center). Whether in or out of the monastery the same standards of discipline and neatness are expected of the monks.

57 (right). A cup of tea is never more appreciated than at times like this.

Work

◁ 58. Time is set aside each day for the monks to clean the monastery grounds. Here, too, the rule of silence prevails.

59. The daily monastic work (*samu*) not infrequently consists of heavy labor such as this.

60. Cleaning the grounds of the monastery graveyard is, naturally, something that must not be neglected. In this instance the graves are those of former roshi of Empuku-ji. The Chinese characters on the center grave denote the date of death of the deceased.

61. The participation of monks in manual labor has been one of Zen's distinguishing characteristics since its conception in China. Here monks chop firewood.

62. The gardens of Zen temples are famous throughout the world. The monks make painstaking efforts to keep Empuku-ji's gardens beautiful.

63. The "Zen life" is and must be expressed as fully in carrying firewood as in the practice of zazen. The deeper the monk's awareness of this fact becomes, the stronger his practice will be.

64. In Japan, where there is an abundant supply, bamboo serves many utilitarian purposes, not the least of which is as clothes poles.

65. Constant rubbing over a period of years with damp cloths produces an almost wax-like gloss on the corridor floors.

66. The kitchen is one of the most important training areas of a Zen monastery. To be assigned as kitchen chief (*tenzo*) is an honor reserved for a monk who has shown great diligence in his training. Together with this honor, however, comes the heavy responsibility to provide food for the community of monks. This food must be both tasty and of sufficient quantity to sustain their training but yet, at the same time, brooking neither luxury nor waste.

67. The monks as
the Zendo. The Ze
only as a place for
zazen but as the
quarters as well.

68. The frugality of monastic life can also be seen in the painstaking patchwork on the sliding paper doors (shoji).

69. Wooden plank ramps, such as these outside the Zendo, are a common means of connecting the various buildings of the monastery.

70. In a recess in the inner part of the Zendo there is an altar at the top of which is enshrined a figure of Bodhidharma, the Indian priest who is said to have brought Zen to China in the early part of the sixth century A.D.

71. As the monks' practice "ripens" they are able to concentrate their minds and become fully absorbed in zazen.

72. Through complete absorption in zazen a monk is able to look deeply into his inner self and discover his "true face."

73. The monks become absorbed in zazen through the consideration of the *koan* which the roshi has assigned to them individually.

74. When a monk becomes lax or drowsy during zazen, a fellow monk will strike him on the back with a long flat stick (*keisaku*) to "encourage" him in his sitting.

75. The pain produced by a blow of the *keisaku* is sharp but of brief duration. The monk pulls down his left shoulder with his right hand in order to protect his shoulder bone from being struck by accident. Both before and after the *keisaku* strikes, both the striker and the struck bow to each other in reverence.

76. The sound of raindrops as they fall upon the rock gutter that surrounds the Zendo is very conducive to zazen.

77. The evening ringing of the large monastery bell (*ogane*) marks the end of the day for the monks.

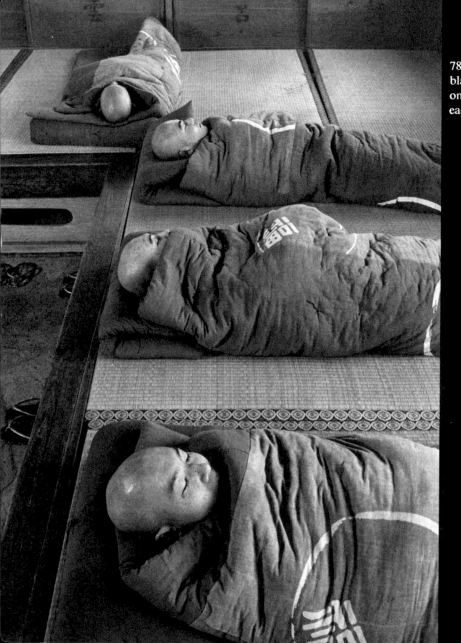

78. Wrapped in *futon* (quilted blankets) the monks go to sleep on the one tatami alloted to each of them in the Zendo.

79. Some monks, however, being particularly earnest in their training, forgo the opportunity to sleep in order to continue zazen.

80. The beauty of Empuku-ji, surrounded as it is by natural forests and bamboo groves, is something which must be seen to be really appreciated.

Head Shaving

81. The mutual shaving of each others' heads is an important religious practice for the monks and is conducted in the Zendo. Since only warm water is used for shaving, the monks must make certain that their straight razors are well sharpened.

82. The monks shave each others' heads at five-day intervals on the so-called 4-9 days (*shikunichi*). The term *shikunichi* derives from the fact that such days fall on the 4th, 9th, 14th, 19th, etc., of each month.

83. *Shikunichi* are used by the monks not only for shaving each others' heads but also for attending other personal needs as well, not the least of which is the mending of robes.

Bathing

84. The Chinese characters read: "The bath is open." On *shikunichi*, with their heads freshly shaven, the monks are able to take their only scheduled bath.

85. In the entryway of the bath is an altar on which a figure of the guardian deity of the bath, Batsudaharashin, is enshrined.

86. As a sign of reverence the monk bows deeply before the guardian deity of the bath. This form of obeisance in Zen is used to aid the monk in realizing humbleness of spirit, thus freeing him from attachment to Self.

87. Whether a monk's specific duty is to prepare food or heat the bath water, he is contributing not only to the maintenance of the whole religious community but also to the realization of his own true Self.

The Joys of Monastic Life

88. These Japanese radishes (*daikon*) are hung up to dry, later to be used to make a type of pickle (*takuan*) for which Empuku-ji is famous.

89. After having been left to dry for more than two weeks the *daikon* are ready to be pickled.

90. Before pickling, however, the *daikon* must be thoroughly cleaned and cut to appropriate lengths.

91. The *daikon* glow in the
rays of the winter sun.

92. Many heads of Chinese cabbage (*hakusai*) waiting to be pickled are also piled up in a corner of the kitchen.

93. After the *daikon* are ready for pickling they are placed in wooden tubs and salt is sprinkled on them. Later, as the pickling progresses, large rocks are placed on the tub lids for several months until the pickles are ready.

94. In the pickling room (*tsukemono-beya*) a monk uses heavy stones to compress the vegetables. Making pickles in the traditional manner not only takes a great deal of preparation but some of brawn as well.

95. As the year draws to a close the monks make rice cakes (*mochi*) to greet the New Year's season.

96. Rice must be specially steamed to make it suitable for being pounded into *mochi*. The monks assigned to the kitchen are especially busy at *mochi*-making time.

97. All the food served in a Zen monastery is vegetarian, and after a particularly large religious observance the monks enjoy a change from their normal diet, being served *udon* (wheat-paste noodles).

98. Before being eaten the *udon* is dipped in a very nutritive and delicious sauce containing such varied ingredients as dried and seasoned laver (*nori*), sea tangle (*kombu*), grated *daikon*, stock made from dried mushrooms, sesame seeds (*goma*), finely chopped green onions, ginger, etc.

99. These banners announce the first religious observance of the New Year at Empuku-ji to honor Bodhidharma. Many laymen from the surrounding area will also come to worship at this time.

100. This stone marker stands beside a pine tree that is closely connected with Nantembo, a famous Zen priest of the Edo period (1603–1868).

101. This scene calls to mind the famous *koan:* "Does a puppy possess the Buddha-nature?"

THE ZEN LIFE

Part II: A COMMENTARY

1 · The Tradition and Creativity of Zen

Zen has its origin in India and was introduced to China where it united with the thought of Lao-tsu and the realistically oriented world outlook of the Chinese, stressing as it does the value of human labor. Zen further developed by incorporating the Confucian emphasis on etiquette and culture, reaching its zenith in the period from the T'ang through the Sung dynasty (618–1279). It was transmitted to Japan in the Kamakura period (1185–1336) where it not only contributed to the disciplining of the spirit of the emotionally prone Japanese people but also deeply influenced the military and fine arts as well as daily life in general.

Professor Hajime Nakamura of Tokyo University, in his *Gendai Zen Koza* (Lectures on Modern Zen), has made a study of the way in which the life of monks changed when Zen was brought to China from India. In the India of the Zen sage Bodhidharma's day, around the sixth century A.D., it was the general practice for monks to live through mendicancy, just as it still is in the countries of Southeast Asia to this day. Even after Zen was brought to China, it is thought, this Indian way of life

was generally followed until at least the time of the third successor, or patriarch, after Bodhidharma, Seng-ts'an. The fourth patriarch, Tao-hsin, after having wandered for ten years, settled down to live in one temple for a period of more than thirty years during which time seekers of the Way came to train under him from every part of the country, numbering generally more than five hundred at any one time. This number further increased to a thousand under the fifth patriarch, Hung-jen, producing new conditions for Chinese Zen. That is to say, if such a large number of monks were to study Zen in the mountains, as was the Chinese practice, it is only natural that they would try to become self-sufficient since there were no cities nearby that could supply their needs through mendicancy. In the hot climate of South Asia both food and clothing are no problem, since one can sleep almost naked under the trees and sustain oneself by eating wild fruit. In the severe climate of North Asia this is impossible. As the priests in South Asia do not do any manual labor, they are able to make do with only one meal a day, but in China this system is impossible.

Even in the collection of regulations of the Zen sect written in the T'ang dynasty (618–907) by the Chinese Zen master Pai-chang, provision is made for two daily meals: breakfast, consisting of rice gruel, and lunch, consisting of vegetables and rice. Later on, even an evening meal known as *yaku seki* (baked stone)[1] came to be tacitly permitted.

At any rate, as Zen became popular in China and was united with that country's culture, it came to place a high value on manual labor and productive activities, both of which had become necessary for its continued growth. By the time of the sixth patriarch, Hui-neng, it is recorded, monks were polishing rice as well as cutting firewood. That is to say, at this time manual labor had become an essential part of Zen training. The Zen master Pai-chang (720–814), whose *Ching-kuei* (Monastic Regulations) forms the model for Zen communal life, set the example himself for this kind of life by participating in manual labor with the other monks even in his old age. This was in accordance with his famous expression, "If one does not do any work for a day, one should not eat for a day." The Zen goal of living life with an "ordinary mind" may be said to have been developed through a life such as this.

The rules and regulations to be followed in a monastery were transmitted to Japan at the same time Zen was. Dogen-zenji (1200–53),[2] the founder of the Soto Zen sect in Japan, particularly made these clear in such works as the *Tenzo Kyokun* (A Guide to the Kitchen Supervisor), *Bendoho* (Rules for the Practice of the Way), *Chiji Shingi* (Regulations for Monastery Officials), *Fujuku Hampo* (Rules for Preparing Food), and *Shuryo Shingi* (Rules for the General Body of Monks). All of these works have as their foundation the Soto Zen teachings of *shikan-taza* (themeless zazen) and *igisoku buppo* (one's bearing is the Buddhist teaching). The Soto Zen tradition has been transmitted fairly faithfully down to the present day.

The Rinzai Zen sect, on the other hand, has undergone a number of changes since it was first introduced into Japan, these changes being fully recorded by Shikyo-osho in his work, *Ganshin-dojo Shishu* (The Purpose of the Ganshin-dojo). As a disciple of Byakuin it was he

---

[1]This expression came into being in the period before evening meals were served and refers to the heated stones the monks held against their stomachs to overcome feelings of hunger and cold.

[2]Zenji, kokushi, osho, daishi, and roshi are all honorific titles given to Japanese Zen priests.

who was responsible for the construction of monastic facilities at Empuku-ji, which were open to anyone who desired to study the Way. Rinzai Zen, which had also been transmitted to Japan in the Kamakura period, had originally established itself with five main and seven subsidiary temples under the protection of the emperor and the Hojo and Ashikaga families. In a short period of time there came to be hundreds of monks living at these temples and the various rules and regulations were being followed in a very rigorous manner.

By the end of the Ashikaga era (1392–1573), however, the five main temples were only ghosts of their former selves, the Rinzai Zen tradition continuing to flourish only at Daitoku-ji, and Myoshin-ji, under the respective leadership of Daito and Kanzan and their descendants. But even though the tradition continued in medieval times, facilities for training monks disappeared at even these two temples and their head priests served on the basis of a yearly rotation system. Although the Zen masters in these two temples were superior to those in the provinces, because their facilities were quite limited it was impossible for them to give training to the novice monks who assembled from all over the country. It was in such circumstances that the Zen master Shikyo-zenji decided to invite virtuous monks, in whom various Rinzai Zen masters placed high hopes, to gather together. According to his plan such priests, without regard to their backgrounds, would then undergo training in a monastery where the head priest would have a tenure of three to five years and the discipline would be the strictest in the Rinzai Zen sect. Finally Shikyo's plan bore fruit, and, revering Daio-kokushi as the founder of the temple, monastic facilities were reestablished at Empuku-ji.

There are some people who think that the reason monastic facilities fell into such a sad state of disrepair in medieval times was because Rinzai Zen put so much emphasis on practicing zazen while using *koan* and because it was so organizationally divided, with its priests continually engaged in making pilgrimages to visit various masters. But according to Shikyo's *Purpose:* "If only one has the correct aspiration, one should be able to practice zazen even in a noisy crowd. However, there are those in the present age who, although they cannot be said to be particularly excellent, will awaken to a desire for the Way if they see a monastery where the rules are being strictly observed. There are also those in whom a desire to realize the Truth will be brought about through the collective strength of the community of monks in their earnest practice of the Way. The nature of what one sees and hears in a monastery is like that of walking through a mist. That is to say, it penetrates through one naturally, leaving a deep impression. Especially in the present degenerate age of *mappo*[3] the merit arising from this nature is not to be taken lightly. With these reasons serving as the core, and putting particular emphasis on ancient practices, I would like to establish a monastery."

Because of Shikyo the facilities of Rinzai Zen monasteries gradually improved, but it can be said that the rules and regulations followed there are today, in comparison with those in Soto Zen, somewhat simplified and practical in nature.

The Zen life is not something which remains unchanged in spite of changes in customs, time periods, nationalities, cultures, and traditions. On the contrary, it is exactly in its adaptation to such changes that Zen expresses its creativity. It is for this reason that there is room left for new growth on the part of Zen in the present age as well.

2 · The Monastic Training of Past Zen Masters

In order to understand monastic training thoroughly it is necessary to study not only its history but also to look back upon the life of past Zen masters. At this point, by way of recalling past Zen masters, I would like to recount several episodes from the lives of Nantembo-roshi, who initiated Zen training at Empuku-ji at the end of the Edo period (1603–1868), and Sogaku Harada-roshi, a Soto Zen master who trained at Rinzai Zen monasteries in the latter part of the Meiji era (1868–1912).

Nantembo-roshi was born in the reign of Emperor Ninko (1817–46) and died in 1924 at the age of eighty-four. He was a man of magnificent physique with great force of character, who became famous for working havoc on the monasteries of his day, even going so far as to suggest the reexamination of fellow Zen masters. This notable priest, under whose guidance General Maresuke Nogi, of Russo-Japanese War fame, is said to have practiced zazen, began his own training at the age of eighteen. It was then that he went to Empuku-

[3]Tradition says that the Buddhist Law will go through three periods, the last of which, *mappo*, the age of degeneration, will last for ten thousand years.

ji, and after waiting two full days in the entry-way he was allowed to enter the *tankaryo* waiting room, where his desire to participate in Zen training was further tested for a period of one week. Finally he was allowed to enter the Zendo, and he was given the Mu *koan*[1] to solve by his master Sekio-osho.

In the spring of the same year, to commemorate his entry into Empuku-ji, Nantembo planted a pine tree by the side of a well located between the Hondo and the hall to commemorate Bodhidarma. He is said to have made the following oath: "The question is whether or not I will die before this pine tree withers away. Even if this pine tree should wither away, I am determined not to die before I reach the age of eighty." He lasted longer than that, and the pine tree remains healthy to this day. In 1911 a group of interested people built a fence around it and erected a stone memorial marker.

Three years after the oath taking Sekio-osho died, and Nantembo transferred to Bairin-ji (in Kurume, Fukuoka Prefecture), where he trained under Razan-osho. There were more than 128 *unsui* in training there, and it is said that for the next six years Nantembo never slept on his *futon*. At night, after the officials of the monastery had made their inspection, he would quietly put his *futon* away and steal off to the gravesite of the Arima family, which was located on the mountain behind Bairin-ji. There he would continue zazen in winter as well as summer. Sometimes, while sitting in the zazen position in the winter, snow piled up like a miniature mountain on the palms of his hands, but he took not the least heed of it, thinking of how the second Chinese patriarch, Hui-k'o (487–593), had been willing to cut off his own arm in order to study the Way. It is also said that Nantembo did zazen for three years near a well called Bottomless Well. After practicing zazen in this way for a number of years, Nantembo-roshi said, "Simply doing zazen in one place is not sufficient. As one step in Zen training it is necessary to go on a pilgrimage to visit various Zen masters, otherwise one's training cannot be considered complete. Experiencing various difficulties in the course of one's travels is also something which is very valuable. I don't think I am a particularly outstanding priest nor is my understanding of Zen unsurpassed throughout the land, but I

---

[1] This *koan* concerns Chao-chou, a famous Zen priest of the T'ang dynasty. One day some monks asked him in all seriousness, "Does a dog have the Buddha-nature?" Chao-chou answered, "Mu (nothing)." The "solution" to this *koan* consists in comprehending what is meant by this answer.

can say that the reason I came to be held in high esteem by society in general is that I made a pilgrimage to visit twenty-four Zen masters."

Sogaku Harada-roshi was a master of the Soto Zen sect who was the head of Hosshin-ji (near Obama, Fukui Prefecture). I had heard about the severity of the training at this monastery from an American professor of philosophy, Dr. Bernard Phillips, and had hoped to have the opportunity to visit it. At Hosshin-ji a distinctive type of guidance was being given in which Harada-roshi used the *koan* of Rinzai Zen as well as that sect's emphasis on realizing enlightenment. According to the roshi's autobiography, *Daiun Sogaku Jiden,* the first real Zen monastery he entered was Shogen-ji, (near Ibuka, Gifu Prefecture). After having trained there for three years he entered what is now the Soto Zen sect's Komazawa University and, upon graduation, became the head priest of a small temple. Six years later, however, he returned to his alma mater as a research student and studied under such famous Soto Zen scholars as Sotan Oka and Kodo Akino. But because he could not find satisfaction in such scholarly study, he once more entered a Rinzai Zen monastery, this time Nanzen-ji (in Kyoto), where he trained for three years under Dokutan-roshi.

At the end of this period he was called back to Komazawa University and there he spent the next twelve years as a professor. At the request of the residents of his home province he became the head priest of Hosshin-ji and built monastic facilities there in 1922. At its most flourishing time, between about 1929 and 1941, there were always between sixty and seventy monks in training. During the intensive periods of zazen known as *sesshin* a large number of priests and laymen from throughout the country would come to Hosshin-ji; one year, during *rohatsu dai sesshin,*[2] numbering more than 120 persons. Among the products of this monastery are such distinguished priests as Haku'un Yasutani and Horyu Ishiguro.

In 1961, at the age of ninety-one, Harada-roshi passed away. Before continuing with this account of his life, however, I would like to quote a long passage from his autobiography, in which he describes his life at the Rinzai Zen monastery Shogen-ji, where he first began his training as a priest. He writes, "I went to Shogen-ji accompanied by my

---

[2] *Rohatsu dai sesshin,* commemorating the enlightenment of Sakyamuni, the historical Buddha, is held yearly from the first of December to the morning of the eighth.

monk friend, Ryokai Kuritani, whom I had invited to go along with me. New arrivals are usually kept waiting in the entryway for a week, but in our case we were allowed to enter the *tankaryo* after only three days, perhaps because we had come from another Buddhist sect. Our time in the *tankaryo* was also unusually short, being only five days. The head priest was Daigi Ummuken-roshi, and the monastery was flourishing with about ninety-five *unsui* in training. I had heard about this monastery's reputation for severe discipline and had come prepared for the worst. After seeing it for myself, what surprised me more than anything else was the simplicity of the meals. I was raised in a poor temple and was quite used to plain food, but here the morning and evening meals consisted of gruel and *tsukemono* (Japanese-style pickles). The gruel was known as 'ceiling gruel' because it consisted primarily of barley and was so watered down that the ceiling was reflected in it. In order to prepare it, water was first boiled in a large pot into which barley that had been dried and ground into flour with a stone mortar was mixed. The result was a smooth, almost drinkable substance that looked just like muddy water. Served with this were a few pickled vegetables.

"In the fall, when *daikon* were abundant, the neighboring farmers would make generous donations of them to us. Our pickles were made either from the leaves of these daikon or those which the farmers threw away. These leaves were put in vats and sprinkled with salt at several different stages in the pickling process. When they were ready to be eaten, the monk in charge of this work would take them out beside the Zendo and carefully cut up a week's supply for the monk community, piling the pickles up in a large basin. Because of their saltiness they would last a whole week without growing moldy.

"Lunch consisted of cooked grain that was actually almost all barley rather than rice, although there were times when rice, amounting to about ten percent of the total, was mixed in. In addition, there was *miso* (bean paste) soup into which vegetables grown in the nearby fields were put. . . .

"There is an instructive anecdote about the vegetables used in our soup that I would like to tell. This episode occurred before I underwent Zen training and concerns the famous Settan-roshi, who is better known as Thundering Settan. Every night without anyone knowing how they got there, vegetables for the next day's *miso* soup would appear washed and nicely cut in a bamboo basket in the kitchen. Settan-roshi thought that there was no doubt that whoever was doing this was one of the *unsui* in training at the monastery, but he wondered who this commendable person might be. By disguising himself as a monk going out to practice night zazen in the monastery grounds, he discovered that a monk by the name of Tairyo was going to a nearby river and collecting the leaves which the local farmers had discarded in the process of washing their *daikon*. These Tairyo secretly brought to the kitchen. At that time Settan-roshi thought to himself, 'This is the person who should be my successor.' Later on, Tairyo did, as Settan had hoped, succeed him. This is a famous episode, which is told even today as proof of the fact that Zen training by itself is not enough: it must be accompanied by development of character as well. Young novice priests of today should take care to remember this point."

In *The Training of the Zen Buddhist Monk*, Daisetz Suzuki called one of his chapters "Life of Service" (in Japanese, *intoku,* literally, "secret goodness"). This "secret goodness" means to do acts of goodness of which others are unaware. To do good for the sake of goodness, to do good while forgetting goodness— this is Zen training.

Let me return to Harada-roshi's autobiography, for he also has something to say about this subject. "I would like to relate an episode I experienced at Shogen-ji concerning one expression of secret goodness on the part of a novice monk. At that time if a monk simply left his dirty clothing in the washtub, before he knew it someone would have washed them quite clean and dried them. One could not help being deeply appreciative of this, especially since it didn't make any difference whether the dirty garments were underwear or whatever. In addition, after it became dark there were monks who, taking care that they were unobserved, would be striving for the honor of cleaning the toilets."

Relating an account of the severity of his monastic training (which was no less than that administered during the Edo period of Nantembo-roshi's time), Harada-roshi says, "Some of the other monks and I would go out into the monastery grounds to practice zazen every night. Sometimes I would sit in the snow, and other times I would sit in a mosquito-filled bamboo grove or a similar place. It might be said that I underwent severe training; but, actually, if you put your whole heart and soul into it, then even if it's cold or you are being bitten by insects it isn't a hardship."

Harada-roshi has also written an interesting account of his own experience of *satori* (enlightenment), but I think it would be better to refer to it later on. Since we have now deepened our understanding of monastic life, I would like, at this point, to return to a discussion of the monastery itself.

3 · Entering a Zen Monastery

With the exception of Kennin-ji, which is located near the central Gion district, Kyoto's Zen temples, such as Nanzen-ji, Daitoku-ji, Myoshin-ji, Tenryu-ji, Tofuku-ji, etc., are all located in what used to be the suburbs of that city. It is thought that in the past the precincts of these temples were much larger than they are today, that the surrounding area was not crowded with houses, and that although they may not have been exactly secluded spots they did at least maintain a certain tranquillity. Recently, however, their precincts have become quite confined, they are crowded in by houses, and they are becoming ghosts of their former selves.

An exception to this is Empuku-ji, which was rehabilitated by Shikyo-osho in the middle of the Edo period. This monastery, located at the foot of Mount Nan, approximately three and a half miles from Yahata Station on the Keihan Railway Line, has been able to preserve its peaceful atmosphere. Leaving the main road one passes through bamboo groves, and after walking uphill on a narrow path for fifteen minutes one comes to the Sammon Gate. On each flank of the Sammon is a statue of a Nio (Guardian King), glaring fiercely at monastery visitors. One is reminded of Shozo Suzuki, who began his study of Zen after having been a samurai and who taught Nio Zen, a form in which one does away with all laxness, giving oneself over completely to the strenuous practice of zazen. Standing in front of the entryway to the monastery complex, one notices the modern-looking patchwork design on the tightly closed shoji (paper sliding doors). This design is not something that was planned, rather it is the natural result of the Zen tradition of attaching great importance to even a small piece of paper. That is to say, when the shoji need to be repaired, only the section where the paper has been damaged is replaced, not the entire covering of the door frame.

Cautiously opening the shoji one notices that the entryway is well cleaned, with not a speck of dust to be seen. At the bottom of a wooden pillar there is a sign which reads, "It is forbidden to leave straw sandals in a disorderly manner." "Watch your step" is another sign that is also seen in the entryway of Zen temples. The day we visited Empuku-ji we were amused when, standing in the entryway asking for permission to enter the monastery, a deep voice answered us, saying, "Who is it?" using words spoken in a traditional Japanese play. If it is someone like us, we simply give the priest who comes to greet us one of our visiting cards and explain to him that we already made an appointment by telephone to meet the roshi. When a novice monk desires to enter Empuku-ji to train there, however, it is not such a simple matter. First of all he must undergo a severe examination.

A Zen monastery is not a place where just anyone may train, but rather its doors are open to only those who earnestly aspire to study the Way. Zen masters take the attitude that "it is quite sufficient to train a single person only or even one-half a person who has truly understood the essence of Zen and is fit to be their successor." Bodhidharma did not consent to instruct his eventual successor, Hui-ko, until the latter had shown his strong desire to study the Way by cutting off his own arm. In Japan this incident has become well-known through the famous paintings of Ses-shu, the best known Japanese artist-priest of medieval times.

As has already been mentioned in the foregoing descriptions of the training of various Zen masters, the entrance test which novice monks must undergo in modern monasteries consists, first of all, in being kept waiting in the entryway and, second, in being placed in the *tankaryo,* where the monk does nothing but zazen under the constant surveillance of senior monks.

Tsuguo Miyajima, a writer who entered the Buddhist priesthood at the age of forty-five, has vividly described his entrance into a Zen monastery in a number of books he has written, particularly *Zen ni Ikiru* (Living in Zen) and *Unsui ga Kataru* (A Novice Monk Speaks). In the latter he writes: "After stepping into the entryway, the *unsui* stands his wicker hat up against the wall in a corner of the room. Then he sits down on the wooden step of the porch and places his baggage, containing his robes and personal effects, in front of him. Next, after taking his entrance application out of his pocket, he inclines his body forward, placing his forehead on top of his hands which are already resting on his baggage. Having thus readied himself, the *unsui* at last makes his presence known to the monastery officials. After a voice from inside the monastery building asks, "Who is it?" a monastery official comes out to the entryway and, kneeling on the floor, asks, "Where have you come from?" The *unsui* gives the official his entrance application and says, "I came from such-and-such temple and am a disciple of so-and-so roshi. I have come with the desire to train here." "Wait just a moment," the official answers and disappears inside the monastery building. Assuming his original position the *unsui* must wait without making the slightest movement until another official comes out and says something like, "As this monastery is completely filled now, we can't take any more trainees" or "Since the discipline here is very severe it would be better for you to go somewhere else." Being refused in this way is a traditional Zen practice, and if the *unsui* gives up at this point, he will never be accepted as a trainee anywhere he may go. There is no other way for him but to continue earnestly requesting admittance by remaining seated, head down, on the porch step. This is known as *niwazume* (being kept in the garden).

If, during the period of *niwazume*, the novice monk asks any questions or acts imprudently, the monastery official will say, "How dare you think of training here when you act in such a manner. Get out!" and then proceed to throw the *unsui*, bag and baggage, out of the entryway, closing the shoji tightly behind him. At any rate, if he really wants to enter the monastery there is nothing for the *unsui* to do but maintain the same bowing posture. However, it is the general practice for him to be given meals during the time he is waiting, although after he finishes eating he must resume his original position. At times during his waiting period one of the monastery officials will come out to heap abuse on him and try to throw him out of the entryway. When evening arrives he will be told that he can stay in the *tankaryo* for the night, although he will have to leave early the next morning. He will also be provided with supper.

Early the next morning the *unsui* resumes the same bowing posture as on the previous day. As time passes his body begins to hurt all over, and his face, legs, and other parts of his body gradually become swollen. On the evening of the second day, after subjecting him to abusive language once again, the monastery official will say, "As you seem to be earnest in your desire to enter, we will put you in the *tankaryo*. However, if you think that everything will be all right now and relax your effort, you can be thrown out at any time." For the next three to seven days, depending on the earnestness shown by the *unsui* in doing zazen, he will be kept in the *tankaryo.* It is only after successfully completing this probationary period that he is allowed to become a member of the monastic community.

The hardest training that takes place in a Zen monastery during the year is known as the *rohatsu dai sesshin,* an intensive period of zazen lasting from the first of December to the morning of the eighth, that commemorates the enlightenment of the historical Buddha, Sakyamuni. The word "sesshin" means to concentrate one's mind. This is accomplished through day and night practice of zazen and private interviews with the roshi during the week-long period. In addition to *rohatsu* other *sesshin* are held every month from the first to seventh, eleventh to seventeenth, and twenty-first to twenty-seventh day during the summer and winter *ango* (training periods). During the intervals between *ango* the monks are allowed to make pilgrimages or return to their home temples. During the training periods the 1st, 3rd, 6th, 8th, 11th, 13th, 18th, 21st, 23rd, 28th, and 31st are set aside for lectures on Zen; from the 2nd, on every third day is for mendicancy; and the 4-9 days (i.e., those in which the figure 4 or 9 appears) are for bathing and head shaving.

The normal daily routine varies somewhat according to the monastery, but, taking Kyoto's Sokoku-ji as an example, the monks schedule generally follows this pattern. The monks rise at 3 A.M., quickly rinse out their mouths with one scoopful of water, wash their faces and immediately begin the morning sutra recitation. Following this they have an opportunity to have a private interview with the roshi; those monks not doing so practice zazen. Breakfast is next, followed by zazen and daily cleaning. On days set aside for them, lectures begin from 7 A.M. in the summer and 8 A.M. in the winter. On days for mendicancy, the monks leave the monastery immediately after the daily cleaning. The midday meal is served at 10 A.M. on lecture days and at 11 A.M. when the monks have been out practicing mendicancy. Following lunch the monks may do zazen individually until 1 P.M., when the manual labor period begins. This manual labor, continuing until 3 P.M. in winter and 4 P.M. in summer, is followed by the evening sutra recitation. The evening meal is eaten at 3:30 P.M. in winter and 4 P.M. in summer. As dusk falls, evening zazen begins, and the monks once more have the opportunity to visit the roshi in his room. The day formally ends at 8 P.M. in winter and 9 P.M. in summer, although not until 10 P.M. during *sesshin.* Truly, a monastic day is a full and earnest one.

The following episode happened more than

forty years ago when Dr. Shigenao Konishi, former head of Kyoto University, was living very near Sokoku-ji. At that time he often visited this monastery to hear Daiko Yamazaki-roshi give lectures on Zen. One day, however, an *unsui* asked Dr. Konishi of what use it was to him to listen to a lecture by someone like Yamazaki-roshi, who lacked an academic education. The doctor answered that he thought that there was something very precious in the way in which the roshi put his body and soul completely into his lectures with overflowing compassion, hoping that he would be of assistance in opening the aspirant's "mind's eye" to the Truth. He also said that he found something very valuable in the monastery's severe rules and regulations, its atmosphere, and the *unsuis*' truly polished and well-regulated practice, something that he could not experience at the university. He went on to say that he felt grateful that he lived close to Sokoku-ji and had been given the opportunity to study Buddhism. Dr. Konishi was the same age as Yamazaki-roshi, and they enjoyed a close relationship with one another. When the doctor passed away shortly after the end of World War II Yamazaki-roshi keenly felt the loss of this good friend.

4 · Zazen: Method and Practice

Although zazen is certainly not all there is to Zen, a Zen which lacks zazen may be said to be no Zen at all. It is possible to become aware of one's true Self through ritual invocation of the name of Amida Buddha as practiced in the Komei-kai (Bright Society) of the Jodo sect of Buddhism, but that is not Zen. Enlightenment or *satori* is important, but if one quits practicing zazen after having experienced *satori* once or twice, then that *satori* will not endure for long. The strength that comes from complete absorption in zazen can only be developed by the continuous practice of zazen.

Zazen is a practice which regulates one's body, regulates one's mind, and leads to an experiencing and awareness of one's true Self. To regulate one's body means to straighten one's posture and control one's breathing. Dr. Masumi Chikashige was a professor of the science faculty of Kyoto University who studied Zen under Dokutan-roshi of Nanzen-ji. During the Meiji and Taisho eras (1868–1926) he made a number of interesting studies of Zen from the standpoint of a scientist, many of which were published in book form. He states that sitting cross-legged while straightening one's backbone was not only an effective posture from the standpoint of mental alertness but it was appropriate for meditation over a long period of time as well. Sitting cross-legged with the foot of each leg over the thigh of the other in the full-lotus position, is the posture which gives the body its greatest stability while, at the same time, providing the basis for complete absorption into zazen.

In his book *Sanzen Nyumon* (An Introduction to Zen) Sogen Omori-roshi refers to a description by Harumichi Hida, the creator of a new physiological medical treatment, of his observations of the movements of Toin Iida-roshi as he practiced zazen. With deep admiration Hida says, "After Toin-roshi effortlessly crossed his legs in the full-lotus position, he gradually began to move the upper part of his body. Little by little the roshi's body seemed to rise up. At the moment he lowered the physical focal point of his body to a point located in the center of his clasped hands, his body movement stopped abruptly, and he seemed to be as massive as great Mount Tai of China. How impressive his majestic manner, imperturbability, merciful countenance, commanding presence, inviolability!"

Koryu Osaka-roshi, among others, has also taught that, "Once you have achieved the basic zazen posture, you should move the upper part of your body to the right and left, front and back, two or three times. When you feel as though you are a giant pillar attached to the earth's axis and supporting the heavens, you should sit composedly yet massively." In *Zazen Yojinki* (Points to Watch in Zazen) the Soto Zen master Keizan Shokin says, "When you have quieted your mind and body, you should sit in grand majesty." What makes this possible is the pledge on the part of the doer, based upon the infinite compassion of a Bodhisattva, to continue the practice of zazen until all sentient beings have realized enlightenment. It is this pledge which makes zazen become alive and radiant.

Excellent explanations in Japanese on the methodology and proper mentality for the practice of zazen are numerous, including books by Dogen-zenji and the abovementioned *Zazen Yojinki*. Modern works include those by Omori-roshi, Harada-roshi, and Osaka-roshi as well as my own *Shinri Zen*. In *Zazengi* and Dogen's *Gakudo Yojinshu* emphasis is placed on the practice of zazen not for one's own personal benefit, but rather for the sake of all human beings, which is to say, for the sake of each and every living creature. While arousing within oneself a heart full of infinite compassion one should strive for the salvation of all existence.

Futhermore, in both the *Zazengi* and *Fukan Zazengi* it is written that, "Zazen is the easy way to enter the gate leading to the Buddhist truth." In the *Zazen Yojinki* it is also written that, "A lack of sufficient clothing, food, and sleep are known as the three insufficiencies, these insufficiencies being the cause of slothfulness on the part of monks." These works also point out that "Zazen should be practiced in a place which is neither too bright nor too dark, too hot nor too cold" and that before sitting in 'pleasant' zazen a meditation cushion of ample thickness should be prepared."

The historical Buddha, Sakyamuni, rejected the severe ascetic practices of the Hindu priests of his day. He did, however, advocate moderation in all things, particularly in regard to food and clothing. He warned against becoming attached to luxurious food and recommended that a man only fill his stomach two-thirds of the way full, leaving one-third empty. He taught that beautiful clothing causes greed and a fear of robbers while dirty clothing makes one prone to sickness, thus preventing one's practice of the Way, and therefore, together with the other obstacles, should be avoided. I think it is quite clear that even from today's perspective these teachings are very reasonable.

The Rinzai and Soto traditions for the practice of zazen are different. For example, in Rinzai monasteries the monks do zazen while sitting face to face, although there is a considerable distance between them. In Soto monasteries, however, the monks sit facing the wall, with their backs to one another. For the beginner in zazen facing the wall is useful in concentrating the mind, but if he sits too close it also has the effect of making him feel nervous. In both sects the eyes are kept open during zazen and the eyelids are allowed to drop naturally until one is looking downward at about a forty-five degree angle.

In both sects after a certain period of time all the monks leave their sitting places and begin moving around the Zendo in *kinhin* (walking zazen). In Soto the method of walking is extremely quiet, the monks progressing only one-half of a foot length with each breath. In Rinzai, on the other hand, the monks walk extremely fast. Although Harada-roshi was trained in the Soto method, at his monastery the monks walk at a pace midway between Soto's and Rinzai's.

As a method of mind regulation, Rinzai

Physiological
evidence

recommends the counting of one's breaths during zazen. The chief method of Soto is *shikan-taza* (themeless zazen), but for beginners whose minds are easily disturbed by extraneous thoughts it also teaches that the method of quietly counting one's breaths may be used. Horyu Ishiguro-roshi, who developed Nio (Guardian King) Zen into an effective method of controlling one's mind, is known to have used a kind of *shikan-taza* in which one concentrates on the sensation of doing zazen itself as the final step in realizing enlightenment. This is very close to the Burmese method of meditation. The chief methods of meditation in the Southern Theravada school of Buddhism, of which Burma is a part, are to move the stomach wall in and out when breathing, and to be completely conscious of each and every action one performs such as, for example, the lifting, stretching, and lowering of the foot when walking. It is believed that in this way freedom from discriminative thinking can be achieved. There are also several other methods in this school that I think are of great value in helping to understand the essential aspects of zazen.

Listening to various sounds is a way of achieving total concentration that is used by Indian Yoga and other meditative schools as well as by Zen. I think that the "What is the sound of one hand clapping?" *koan* of Pai-yin is closely related to this method. In the Chinese collection of *koan* known as the *Pi-yen-lu* (Blue Cliff Records) there is a verse to the effect that becoming absorbed in the sound of falling rain is also an extremely good method of concentrating one's mind.

The abovementioned Dr. Chikashige was a pioneer in subjecting Zen to scientific investigation. He had a doctor examine him while he did zazen and it was discovered that the pressure exerted by his abdominal muscles had increased, the movement of his lungs became extremely slow, and, even though a stethoscope was used, his heartbeat could not be detected. In another test he had another doctor seal his mouth and nose for periods up to three hours without his being the least affected. He explained that it was possible for him to do this because, as ancient Zen masters had said, the power arising from being completely absorbed in zazen, caused all 84,000 of his pores to facilitate his breathing. On this basis he advanced a theory that the state of complete absorption in zazen was not unlike that of animals in hibernation. He also went on to say that he thought this could be verified through a urine examination.

Independent of Dr. Chikashige's experiments were those of Professor Saburo Sugiyasu of Tokyo University of Education and his group. They made a study three or four years ago of the change of rate in breathing and metabolism that occurs during zazen. Some other psychologists and I assisted them. We discovered that the number of breaths per minute slows down from sixteen or seventeen to as few as two or three, and the metabolic rate is reduced to approximately eighty percent of what it would be normally. Parallel with our study, Professor Akira Kasamatsu of the Psychology Department of Tokyo University made an investigation into the changes in the brain waves of zazen practitioners. The results of all of these studies have served to support Dr. Chikashige's hypothesis to some extent, although, as yet, no one has made the study of urine analysis he recommended. The fact that zazen and other methods of mind and body control are extremely effective and rational is, however, gradually being made clear through studies such as these.

5 · The Immeasurable Merit of Zazen

Keizan-zenji has written in *Zazen Yojinki* that "with infinite compassion one should transfer the immeasurable merit that derives from one's practice of zazen to all sentient beings." As one becomes experienced in the practice of zazen there is an almost infinite number of resultant good effects. It is these good effects that are to be devoted to the benefit of all existence. Since there is immeasurable merit, I think it is only natural that the particular contents of that merit should differ somewhat according to the circumstances of the viewer. In Dogen-zenji's *Fukan Zazengi* he teaches that, "when you have mastered the essentials [of zazen] your body will naturally become free and easy, your mind will be quick and feel refreshed, your thinking will be clearer and you will realize profound enlightenment."

In my book, *Shinri Zen*, I listed the ten benefits that result from zazen as follows. The practitioner's life is given increased vitality, thereby helping him recover from sickness. His nervous system is better regulated, thereby aiding in the treatment of nervous disorders. His temperament is changed through being cured of either short-temperedness or melancholy. His will becomes stronger. His work efficiency is heightened, and the number of accidents he incurs is reduced. His thinking process is improved and his creative power is

perceptions

increased. His personality becomes more pliable and its integration is advanced. As the "eye" of enlightenment is opened he comprehends the highest conception of man and the world. By standing on life's most basic foundation he can realize a deep peace of mind that opens the way to the world of the enlightened and radiates deep compassion for all existence. In addition to these, I must not forget to mention the highest merit that comes from the practice of zazen, namely, "no merit at all."[1]

In his book, *Sanzen Nyumon,* Omori-roshi also relates the benefits which result from Zen training. Although he has not ignored the physiological effects, he has concentrated more on the attitudes toward life that Zen masters have held since ancient times. Among these he lists a calmness of spirit no matter what the circumstances; "sitting death," i.e., being able to choose to die while doing zazen; the realization that "every day is a fine day"; being able to act spontaneously and without restraint; sitting alone feeling as if one were a high majestic mountain; bringing joy to those around you when passing by; accepting any hardship; acting without concern for public recognition or acclaim; seeing things as they truly are; and a willingness to suffer for the sake of others.

6 · Monastic Work

There is a tendency among various peoples, particularly Indians, to think of Zen as being the same as Yoga, although—it must be admitted—there are some teachers of Yoga in Japan who are quite well informed on Zen. At any rate it should be understood that the character of Zen has been heavily influenced by Chinese culture, one of the most important expressions of which is that culture's respect for labor. As I have mentioned before, the spirit of the words, "If one does not do anything for a day, one should not eat for a day" as expresssed by Pai-chang, is one of the main pillars of the Zen life. Even though Pai-chang was eighty years old or thereabouts, every morning he would go out to work in the fields. His disciples, however, were unable to

---

[1]Translator's note: This denial of merit is used to discourage the Zen aspirant from seeing zazen as a method of fulfilling his self-centered desires, a purpose the very opposite of that which Zen is aiming for.

bear seeing their aged master continue his work in the fields, so one day one of them hid his rake. Because he was not able to work in the fields he sat in his room passing the time tediously, refusing to eat the food that was brought to him. When one of his attendants would say, "Please eat this food," he would answer, "If I don't work for a day, I won't eat for a day."

That other Zen masters beside Pai-chang participated in manual labor can be surmised from this account: One day when Chao-chou was sweeping the garden a priest came to him and asked, "You are famous throughout the land for your great knowledge, so how is it that you are sweeping up the dirt here?" In India, however, it has been the general rule for priests to live through mendicancy while manual labor has traditionally been looked down upon. This attitude is quite strong even in today's India, and, together with the caste system, it forms the stumbling block to that country's reconstruction. But in regard to China, particularly its present Communist government, participation in labor service, even by high government officials, is viewed as being extremely important. This has been a characteristic of the Chinese people from ancient times and is so today.

In Japan a famous episode that has been handed down concerns the founder of Myo-shin-ji, Senkizan-kokushi. When the founder of Tenryu-ji Temple, Muso-kokushi, (who is known as the teacher of seven emperors) was being carried to his home from the imperial palace in a gorgeous palanquin, he happened to pass by Myoshin-ji. In front of the main gate he noticed an old priest sweeping the path with a broom, and upon closer observation he saw that it was Sekizan-kokushi. It is recorded that after they had exchanged greetings with each other and taken their mutual leave, Muso-kokushi remarked that it was certain that Sekizan's disciples would flourish.

Cooking, heating the bath water, gathering and splitting firewood, working in the fields, making Japanese pickles and, of course, cleaning—these are just some of the various types of work that the self-supporting monks carry on. These activities are well portrayed in the photographs appearing in this book. The head priest of Empuku-ji, Soen Tsuzan-roshi, writing in the Buddhist magazine *Dai-horin* at the time when his master, Gempo Yamamoto-roshi of Mishima's Ryutaku-ji, died at the age of ninety-six, said that when he went to visit his master before his death, Yamamoto-roshi asked him whether or not he still contined to clean the toilet. He did, of course, although he was more than seventy.

7 · Zen Training: The Way of Enlightenment

Zen is not simply a matter of sitting quietly. Taishun Sato-roshi, the second most important monastery official of the Soto Zen sect's Eihei-ji, has written quite clearly in *Zen no Igi* (The Meaning of Zen) that, "The essence of Zen is in satori." To realize satori it is particularly important to have the guidance of a qualified Zen master. The master gives lectures in which he expresses his own interpretation and understanding of the Zen classics, thus providing a stimulus for the Zen trainees' own realization of enlightenment. He also encourages the trainees and offers them individualized instruction through personal interviews.

Entering the master's room to seek personal instruction is called *nyushitsu sanzen*. In Rinzai Zen each trainee is given a *koan* such as Chao-chou's Mu or "What is the sound of one hand clapping?" to struggle with. For the monk zazen is not the "pleasant entryway to the Truth" of Soto Zen, but rather what is required of him is that he have "a great doubt," "great determination," and "deep faith." There may be times when he forgets to eat or sleep, or even times when he does not know whether he is dead or alive. Even in ordinary Zen monasteries there are periods of intensive zazen during the year, such as *rohatsu dai sesshin*, when the monks must endure severe cold, make do with only two or three hours of sleep in the zazen position, and devote themselves entirely to finding a "solution" to the *koan* they have been given. Furthermore, it is not a simple task to have a "solution" accepted by the roshi. The trainee must be ready to be thrown out of the master's teaching chambers under a barrage of physical and verbal abuse. If, as a result of this, he hesitates to visit the roshi, then the monastery official who acts as the monks' supervisor will drag him out of the Zendo and force him to go to the roshi's room. He finds himself caught between two fires, not knowing what to do. When he decides he must go, he strikes the small bell at the entryway twice and enters the roshi's room, feeling exactly as if he were entering a lion's den. It is said that in ancient times many monks became sick and even lost their lives as a result of such severe training.

In Byakuin's *Yasen Kanwa* (Night-Boat Tales) he tells how, after very severe training, he realized enlightenment, only to come down with serious damage to his lungs and nervous prostration. Although the doctors gave him up as a hopeless case he made a visit to a religious mountain hermit by the name of Byakugen. This hermit taught him a method of meditative introspection and, miraculously, he recovered. His subsequent devotion to saving others was truly the fruit of this deeply felt experience.

At the beginning of his teaching career Byakuin instructed his students to study the Mu *koan* but later on he came to feel that "What is the sound of one hand clapping?" was a more effective *koan*. He emphasized repeatedly that if Zen trainees would only practice in earnest, they could realize enlightenment in as short a time as three to five days. And one story exists about a man named Heishiro who was able to realize enlightenment and have Byakuin certify his experience as genuine after practicing intense Nio Zen for only three days and nights while confined in the monastery bath.

In most present-day monasteries there is little effort made to promote more efficient methods for realizing enlightenment. Horyu Ishiguro-roshi, a disciple of Sogaku Harada-roshi and founder of the Zen Rigaku-kai (Zen Science Society), did, however, attempt to modernize Zen. Unfortunately he was taken ill while traveling abroad and died a few years ago, but I think his efforts to rationalize Nio Zen are worthy of close consideration.

Even if a trainee is able to pass through the first barriers to full enlightenment comparatively easily, it is necessary for the master to continue to use harsh methods to ensure that the trainee will continue on to higher levels. Realization of enlightenment is not something that can occur only in the Zendo. It is not unusual for this experience to take place while a person is doing manual labor, making a pilgrimage, or practicing mendicancy. Sogaku Harada-roshi has written that he realized enlightenment a second time when he saw the foam of his own urine while on a pilgrimage.

There was a woman by the name of Chiyono who studied Zen under the guidance of Bukko-kokushi. At the time of her enlightenment she wrote the following poem: "Passing through the bottom of the bucket that Chiyono has received, water does not accumulate nor does the moon take shelter." I think she has expressed the substance of the enlightenment experience very well.

Dogen-zenji has stated in his *Fukan Zazengi* that, "One's body and mind will naturally fall away, and one's 'Original Face' (True

Self) will appear." In *Shobogenzo Zuimonki* (A Collection of the Sayings of Dogen-zenji) he went on to say, "If one does zazen for a while one will discover the essence [of Zen] and realize that zazen is the direct approach [to enlightenment]." However, in a passage preceding this Dogen also says, "An ancient master has said, 'Just as one is unaware of one's clothing becoming damp when walking in a fog, so one is unaware of becoming a fine person when one studies under a fine person.' And we know of the account that tells of a child in the service of Gutei-osho who was able to realize enlightenment simply by being near him."

I recently had a discussion with Reirin Yamada-roshi, who served in Los Angeles some years ago as the director of the Soto Zen sect's missionary work in North America. He told me that in Rinzai Zen the trainee studies under a master and *asks* him questions concerning the Buddhist teachings, while in Soto Zen, although the trainee also studies under a master, he is expected to *listen* to his explanations of these same teachings. Rinzai puts primary emphasis on the use of *koan* to achieve enlightenment while Soto makes "themeless zazen" its first consideration. Although both of them do teach that enlightenment is the final goal of Zen, each of them has its own particular way of going about it. Nevertheless, as the methods used by Keizan-zenji (the founder of Soji-ji) show, there are numerous Soto Zen masters who also employ *koan* in their Zen instruction.

Zen attaches particular importance to the transmission of the Buddhist doctrine, or Dharma, from master to disciple. According to Zen doctrine, the historical Buddha, Sakya-muni, first transmitted his enlightenment to his disciple, Kasyapa, who in turn transmitted it to his own disciple, and so on, down to the present day. Dogen-zenji placed particular emphasis on this point. Shindai Seki-guchi of the Tendai sect of Buddhism, however, feels that Bodhidharma is actually an imaginary figure who was created to express the Zen ideal. If this is true, it would mean that there had been an interruption in the line of transmission from Sakyamuni to the present day. On the other hand, since Zen is that which stands in the fountainhead of creativity, it would also mean that it would be possible for Zen itself to be created anew. But whether transmission has been direct or not, in order to prevent what may appear to be enlightenment from being, in reality, merely self-satisfaction, it is important to have an enlightenment experience checked and certified by a genuine master. Furthermore, as has been confirmed by numerous examples, the advice a monk receives from his master after entering the Buddhist priesthood is invaluable.

8 · Religious Mendicancy

Two different Chinese characters can be used to write the "*taku*" of *takuhatsu* (mendicancy), but either way the word means "to hold out a [monk's] bowl with one's hand." The practice of mendicancy was begun by Sakyamuni, and in present-day Japan it has been handed down chiefly as a practice of Zen monasteries. There are certain specified days each month when mendicancy is practiced, and it may be said that the dress of the monks on those days is most appropriate to the name *unsui* (literally, "cloud and water"). They wear the same inner white kimono and outer black robes as always, but on this day they pull up the lower part of their robes and tie the excess cloth securely around their waists with a cord. In addition to white leggings they wear straw sandals and a large wicker hat, with a mendicant's bag completing the outfit. They walk in an orderly fashion, and chant Buddhist sutras as they go. Their voices, coming from deep in their abdomens, serve not only to cultivate their at oneness with themselves but also to spread the spiritual alms of religious exultation among the people. The people are grateful for the service performed by the monks and show their appreciation by giving them material alms. Through mendicancy, both the almsgiver and receiver are mutually immersed in the joy of a practice that leads to enlightenment.

The following verse, I believe, expresses very well the spirit of mendicancy: "There is infinite merit in the giving of spiritual and material alms; such almsgiving produces harmony and completeness." In the Ho'un sutra there is an admonition to practitioners of mendicancy to be extremely careful with regard to the disposition of the material alms they have received. It stipulates that "the material alms received should be divided into four parts: one part being given to one's fellow mendicants, one part to those suffering from hunger, one part to departed spirits, and one part for oneself." And the Hoju sutra promises, "If a man practices mendicancy, all his arrogance will be destroyed." When we consider that it was Sakyamuni himself who provided the model for mendicant practice by begging barefoot, then the meaning of these sutras will become readily understandable.

The description of mendicancy that follows was written by one of the men to whom I have been deeply indebted since my high school days, namely Tokan Hirasawa. After many years of service as the head of the Yamagata Library, he returned to his home temple where he is giving guidance in Zen. A few years ago he participated in an intensive zazen training period at Myoshin-ji, at which time he was also able to practice mendicancy. He told me how glad he was to have had that opportunity. When I asked him to tell me more about the experience, he kindly consented to write the following account.

"Last year, during one of the training sessions at Myoshin-ji, I was able to realize my long-cherished desire to become immersed in the religious exultation of mendicancy. The orthodox style of practicing mendicancy is to do it in a large group, and traditional practice is first consummated when a feeling of mutual trust exists between the almsgiver and receiver. If such a feeling is lacking, then the mendicant will be subject to ridicule by thoughtless individuals and become merely the object of barking dogs.

"It is necessary to practice in an area suit-able for walking in safety and tranquillity. I fear that as more and more high-speed automobiles rush back and forth, it may become impossible to continue this practice, even in such deeply religious cities as Kyoto, where new superhighways have already been built far into the surrounding area.

"I fondly recall the elegance of a poem written by the famous Soto Zen priest of the Edo period, Ryokan-osho. It goes as follows:

Stopping to pick violets,
By the side of the road,
I forgot my begging bowl.
Oh, little bowl, how lonely you must be.

"I was very glad to hear that, because of the influence of Muso Sekizan-daishi, a priest of great virtue, mendicancy at the monastery of Shogen-ji (near Ibuka, Gifu Prefecture) has a tradition of over 600 years. Empuku-ji, which is located in an agricultural area south of Kyoto, has a tradition nearly as long."

The following episode was related to me by Dr. Tsuruji Sahoda, professor emeritus of Osaka University, and a scholar of Yoga. It concerns Somon Horizawa-osho, a person who, while still a student in the economics department of Kyoto University, decided to study Buddhism on Mount Hiei (near Kyoto), and subsequently secluded himself there for the next twelve years. Horizawa has recently begun to practice mendicancy, stopping in front of each house along his way and praying for the happiness of its occupants. He has said that through contact with ordinary people in this way, he has been able to achieve a new state of mind, of a depth he had not been able to achieve through seclusion in the mountains.

Dr. Sahoda also told me about Katai Tayama's novel, *Aru So no Kiseki* (A Certain Priest's Miracle) in which the author describes how a certain priest who practiced mendicancy was able, somehow, to alleviate the disharmony and misfortune in each family before whose home he prayed. While the story is a work of fiction, it is not impossible, I believe, to imagine that a miracle-maker like this one might exist.

Mendicancy not only serves as the Buddhist method through which one is bound to ordinary people, but it can also provide the opportunity for one's own realization of enlightenment. It is said that Byakuin-roshi was able to realize full enlightenment while practicing mendicancy as a monk under the guidance of Keitan Dokyo on Mount Han in Nagano Prefecture. Before that, at the age of twenty-four, he achieved a measure of enlightenment when he heard the sound of the main bell at Eigen-ji, where he was then training. He then became full of himself and took to boasting that there had probably been no one for more than 300 years who had had as penetrating an experience of enlightenment as he. He became so conceited that he began to look upon people as though they were mere clods of earth. It was to this pompous Byakuin that Keitan Dokyo-roshi addressed himself. Because he believed Byakuin held great promise for the future, he was very severe in training him and he put particular emphasis on having him concentrate on "solving" *koan*.

One day when Byakuin was out practicing mendicancy—while at the same time working at his *koan*—he came to a house where an old woman was living. The old woman refused to give him any alms, but still Byakuin refused to move on. This angered the old woman and she took a bamboo broom and brought it down hard on top of the wicker hat he was wearing. Byakuin was hit so hard he fell down and lost consciousness momentarily. Some neighbors saw what happened and rushed to his side to help him. The moment he regained consciousness, Byakuin was immediately able to "solve" the various *koan* he had been given, thus achieving full enlightenment. So excruciating was the experience that he could not help roaring with laughter, and he rushed back to the temple as if he had lost his mind. Keitan took one glance at him and certified that his experience had indeed been genuine. Byakuin was so incomparably happy, the story goes, that he dreamed that night that he saw his mother living happily in Tusita Heaven in Maitreya's inner hall.

9 · The Discipline of Taking Meals

As eating food is the basis for the preservation of human life, it is an important question not only for Zen but also for the general populace. Zen monasteries have their own unique table manners, the rules of which are extremely refined, so much so, in fact, that after the famous Chinese scholar of the Sung dynasty (960–1279), Cheng Ming-tao, visited a Zen temple and saw the solemnity of these manners, he is reported to have said, "The ideals of [Confucian] etiquette are completely expressed therein." Even today these manners have not been forgotten. Their importance can also be seen in the fact that Dogen-zenji wrote two works *Tenzo Kyokun* (A Guide for the Kitchen Supervisor) and *Fujuku Hampo* (Rules for Preparing Food) devoted to a careful explanation of their proper form.

The table manners of Soto Zen retain much of their original form while those of Rinzai Zen have been somewhat simplified. In Rinzai, for example, meals are eaten not in the Zendo but in a separate dining room, while in Soto they are still eaten in the Zendo, using traditional eating utensils, many of which are no longer used in Rinzai. In addition, Soto makes more use of various sounding instruments such as gongs, bells, etc., during the mealtime than does Rinzai, and Soto monks repeat more sutras before and after meals than do their Rinzai counterparts. Both sects do, however, share such common features as the use of various sounding instruments to indicate the various mealtime actions, the prohibition of conversation, the placing of the palms together in the *gassho* gesture at appropriate times, the use of the hands for signaling. In the period before and after the meals, various sutras, such as *Hannya Haramita Shingyo* (the Prajna Paramita Hridya sutra), are recited, blending into a perfect unity with the taking of the meal itself. Representative of the sutras directly concerned with meal taking itself is the following *Gokan no Ge* (Five Reflections Before Eating):

1) Considering the meal's effect, we reflect on whence it came
2) Weighing our virtues, we accept this offering
3) To defend against our delusive minds and separate ourselves from our faults, we must first of all overcome greed
4) To cure our bodily weakness, we take this fine medicine
5) To attain enlightenment, we now eat this food

Although we eat every day, for the most part we do it mechanically, without deep reflection. This is not to say, of course, that we do not sometimes hear people say things like "It was delicious" or "I enjoyed the meal very much." Most people, however, fail to reflect on such things as how many people's beneficence has made it possible for them to eat a particular meal. Where, for example, were the raw materials that go to make up our meals, such as rice, wheat, barley, sugar, vegetables, fruit, etc., cultivated? Or where were they harvested, collected, and processed? How much human effort has been involved? Not only that, but how great a part in this process has been played by the so-called natural forces such as the sun's warmth, the earth's nourishment, the air's action, changes in climate? When it is a question of methods of cultivating rice, or producing other food, not only are the efforts of present-day people involved but those of past ages as well. When we stop to think how the finished foods were transported—for example, how our table sugar, which had previously been cultivated, harvested, processed, and then moved by ship, truck, and other means to the nearby store where we bought it—then we realize that the number of people who have been involved in enabling us to eat is almost infinite. Truly, "considering the meal's effect, we reflect on whence it came."

Considering how great has been the kindness of heaven, earth, and our fellow human beings, we need to ask, "Am I really worthy of receiving the fruit of such cooperation? Have I accumulated such virtue, or moral culture? How apt the saying, "weighing our virtues, we accept this offering."

Zen training is for the purpose of controlling the mind, and curing ourselves of the three primary evil desires: greed, anger, and ignorance. Of these three, however, it must be admitted that greed is the most difficult to overcome. "We must first of all overcome greed" means that when we are about to eat the food that so many people and things have beneficently provided for us, we should be concerned about other human beings who may be starving, and whether or not we are greedily eating that which rightfully belongs to such unfortunates.

Truly, food should be thought of as a medicine to sustain our physical strength. If this is done, then greed will disappear of itself. Thus the expression, "to cure our bodily weakness, we take this fine medicine," was derived.

If we think further about the fundamental nature of this problem, we will come to understand that the reason we are given the opportunity to eat is in order that we may attain the Buddhist Way and realize enlightenment. This might also be expressed as the realization of the four great vows of Bodhisattvahood, beginning with the vow, "to save all sentient beings, however innumerable they may be" and ending with the vow, "to attain the Buddhist Way, however infinite it may be." The vows, expressed more simply, are compressed to, "to attain enlightenment, we now eat this food." The reason the *Gokan no Ge* are recited at Zen mealtimes is none other than to renew the monks' understanding of the meaning of eating and to deepen their vigilance.

At the midday meal the Zen practitioner makes an offering of approximately seven grains of rice. After this he repeats the following sutra: "We offer this food to all hungry spirits." The "hungry spirits" referred to here are not simply those of the departed but embrace all who are suffering from hunger, whether living or dead.

The anecdote that follows concerns Ryuen-osho who was once chief priest of Toko-in in Kobe. Although the *unsui* at the temple would heat the water for his bath, Ryuen-osho refused to bathe in the tub, contenting himself with only two bucketfuls of water for washing his body. His explanation was that the priests had dug a well but had found no water, and because they had to bring water from a distant waterfall, they needed to use it with great care. He also refused to eat more than one serving of food, saying he wished to leave the rest for his descendants to eat. It can truly be said that he made the spirit of providing an offering for "hungry spirits" a part of his daily life.

The monks eat a dish called *o-kayu* (rice gruel) for the morning meal but because this is thirty percent rice and seventy percent barely the name hardly fits.

Zen table manners may resemble those in

the West in the sense that, when eating, monks are not supposed to make any noise, just as Westerners are not supposed to when eating soup. In Zen monasteries though, an exception to this rule is made when the monks eat wheat noodles.

The relationship between Zen and tea is a very deep one. In the monastic regulations formulated by Pai-chang during the T'ang dynasty, there is already a section dealing with the way in which tea should be served. And in Japan, Eisai-zenji, the priest who introduced Rinzai Zen to this country, wrote a work entitled *Kissa Yojoki* (Rules for Improving One's Health through Tea Drinking). The habit of tea drinking became firmly established in Japan in the latter half of the four-teenth century, and it is thought that it spread through the country from the original practice in Zen temples.

It is well known that the Japanese tea ceremony developed with Zen as its background. In present-day monasteries tea is served on such occasions as when there are ceremonies or meetings. Usually the tea which is served has been grown in the monastery fields and is of inferior quality, but when guests come, or on other special occasions, powdered tea is also used. A traditional monastic practice expressing the monks' consideration for others, is the way in which any two monks who happen to be sitting next to each other will place their tea cups close together to make it easier for the person pouring tea.

10 · Zen Food

Since Zen monasteries attempt to be self-supporting in their food requirements through mendicancy and the cultivation of their own vegetable gardens, it follows that their daily meals are extremely plain. However, it is also true that among the vegetarian dishes which have been developed in the Zen sect, there are many which are both delicious and nutritious, although a great deal of time must be ex-pended in their preparation. The Obaku Zen sect's Mampuku-ji, in Uji, Kyoto, is famous for its wide variety of vegetarian food; and the Okutan-style boiled bean curds and other vegetarian dishes served at Nanzen-ji were recently featured in an article in the *The New Yorker*. Itsugai Kajiura-roshi, who is the head priest of Ibuka's Shogen-ji and the president of affiliated Shogen Junior College, is an authority on Zen vegetarian food and has written *Shojin Ryori no Gokui* (The Secrets of Vegetarian Food), a book that tells how to make representative vegetarian dishes, thereby elucidating one of the pleasant aspects of Zen life.

The food served in Zen monasteries is carefully prepared, but it is not luxurious by any means. Seasonal foods, foods which are fully ripe, as well as those foods which happen to be at hand, are eaten. At Kajiura-roshi's monastery he has delicious meals made for the *unsui,* consisting of wild mountain grass and tree leaves as well as horsetail, starwort, dandelion, sorrel, wild butterbur, sprouts, wisteria buds, parsley, trefoil, red beans, etc. He also buys at least one kind of expensive food that the *unsui* would not normally have a chance to eat. It is said that the *unsui* at his monastery are very grateful for the consideration he has shown them.

Another characteristic of Zen monastic food is that none of the materials used in its preparation is to be wasted. It is one of Zen's iron rules that even those parts of the materials which might normally be considerd waste should be used to their fullest. This applies whether the food being prepared is Kenchin-style vegetable soup, vegetable stew, or fried bean curds. Also included in this kind

of food is the Obaku Zen sect's vegetarian dish known as *umpen* (literally, "a piece of cloud"). In this dish, too, all of the scraps are utilized to make liquid starch so as not to waste anything. *Umpen* and *mafu* (bean curd in which sesame seed has been mixed) are the two most characteristic dishes of Obaku Zen. The ingredients for making *umpen* are burdock, carrots, lily bulbs, bamboo sprouts, gingko nuts, green peas, lotus roots, Judas's ear, and mushrooms. To all this is added arrowroot, sugar, and soy sauce, the resulting mixture then being fried in vegetable oil. Gemmyo Murase's book, *Fucha* (Vegetarian Food), includes a nutritional analysis of the food which was served at Obaku sect's Mampuku-ji at the time of a convention held there for the readers of the Japanese-language magazine, *Zen.* The nutritionist who made the analysis said, "Just as I thought, the food served here is extremely nutritious; so much so, in fact, that one meal by itself provides almost one-half of a normal person's daily nutritional needs. . . . Speaking from the standpoint of a specialist, I was most surprised by the high amounts of inorganic salts and vitamins I discovered." He added that, "The use of a large amount of vegetable oil is a characteristic of Chinese-style cooking, of which Zen monastic food is a part. And this is a feature that I would like to recommend from the standpoint of its nutritional value."

Since neither meat nor fish is eaten in a Zen monastery, the monks do not receive any animal protein or fat. However, in place of this they do take in a sufficient amount of high quality vegetable protein and fat through eating such things as soy beans and sesame seeds. However, as soy beans are neither tasty nor easily digestible when eaten in their original form, it is customary to ferment them or change them into either wet or dry soybean curds, thus making them delicious while retaining their nutrition. In addition to curds, the priests also prepare such foods as Suhama-style sweet cakes, made from sugar mixed with soybean flour; Kinzen-ji-style bean paste; and other dishes. Sesame seed is used mixed together with salt to give taste to the morning rice gruel and also as part of the dressing for vegetable salads. Vegetable oil made from either soy beans or sesame seeds is used for frying purposes as well as with other cooked foods. Thus, it can be seen that the nutritional content of monastic vegetarian food is quite sufficient to meet the health needs of the monks.

II · Bathing

The 4th, 9th, 14th, 19th, etc., of each month are set aside for the *unsui* to shave their heads and bathe. On such days the monk in charge of the bath will hang a wooden signboard outside the bath that reads, "The bath is open," informing the other monks that they may bathe. The chief priest of the monastery is the first to bathe, followed by the other monks in an order determined by such factors as their position in the temple, their length of training, etc. Before bathing the monks first show reverence to a statue of Batsudabara (Batsudaharashin), the guardian deity of the bath, by prostrating themselves before it three times. According to tradition this deity is said to have achieved enlightenment as he was about to bathe.

The *unsui* take turns washing each other's backs, and when a monk is having his own back washed he shows his gratitude by placing his palms together in the *gassho* position. The bath that is taken on December 8, at the end of the special week-long period of intensive zazen known as the *rohatsu dai sesshin,* is prepared by the officials of the monastery themselves, and they also wash the backs of the *unsui* to show their appreciation for their efforts.

The fuel used to heat the bathwater consists of fallen leaves, wood chips, and whatever waste material happens to be available. As I have mentioned previously, in Zen nothing must be wasted or used carelessly. The object of learning Zen is, in essence, to save all sentient beings; but, at the same time, it is to become grateful for the many favors we receive from all beings as well. By the favors received from all beings is meant the realization of how our own existence is sustained by all things, thus becoming grateful for their support and cooperation. In the Zen storytelling tradition there are numerous stories concerning Zen masters who have scolded their disciples for having used even insignificant things carelessly.

On Mount En in the outskirts of Okayama City there is a large Zen monastery by the name of Sogen-ji that was, in ancient times, the family temple of Lord Ikeda, a ruler in the Kan'ei era (1624–44). During the final years of the Edo period (1603–1868) and extending into the first part of the Meiji era (1868–1912) there was an outstanding priest by the name of Gizan-osho whose fame was known throughout the country and in whose monastery there was an exceedingly large number of *unsui*. The following story concerns a young *unsui,* Demmoku, who came from the Kyoto area and served as Gizan-osho's personal attendant. One summer evening Gizan-osho entered the bath and, finding it too hot, he called for cold water to be brought. In response to his request Demmoku threw out the small amount of water that was left in the wooden bucket and was about to go to fetch some more when suddenly Gizan-osho yelled in a voice that fell like a bolt of lightning, "You fool, each thing has its use whether it be big or small! Why don't you try to make the best use of things? Won't even a little water serve a useful purpose if it is poured on plants or trees? Don't you know about secret acts of goodness? You foolish priest who lacks the desire for enlightenment!"

Gizan-osho was famous for his sharp temper, but Demmoku took his scolding to heart and chose the words "one drop of water" as his motto. Eventually, after long years of training, he adoped them as his own name: Tekisui. In the first part of the Meiji era, he became a very well-known priest, and served as the head priest of Tenryu-ji. The Buddhist verse he wrote just before his death reads as follows:

In my more than seventy years of life
I have not been able to exhaust
That one drop of water of Sogen-ji
That covers both Heaven and Earth.

Many Japanese tend to forget the value of such things as water. When there is a water shortage, however, as there has been in recent years in cities like Tokyo and Nagasaki, they realize how important even a little water is. And when we consider water, we need to think not only of volume but of quality as well. If we remember that in many parts of the world the water is unfit for drinking unless it is boiled first, then we can appreciate the value of our country's pure water.

12 · Sleep

In *Zazen Yojin Setsu* (Points to Watch in Zazen) a want of sleep is listed as one of the three wants that are the cause of a monk becoming lax in his training. During periods of intensive zazen, such as *rohatsu dai sesshin,* the monks are only allowed to sleep for two or three hours a day with this sleep itself being done while sitting in the zazen position. Once a person becomes used to it, sleeping while in the zazen position is a very efficient method for enabling the mind to recover from fatigue.

Shinkichi Takahashi, who as a youth was famous as a poet of the Dadaist school and later entered the Zen priesthood, has written about his experience during *rohatsu dai sesshin* as follows: "Upon returning home, after having passed a week without having slept while lying down, I hate to spread the *futon* on the floor and sleep on them. It's been said that people in ancient times did not sleep in a horizontal position for periods of up to thirty or forty years. and the Buddhist patriarchs in India are said not to have lain down during their entire lives. I realize now that these stories are not necessarily fabrications."

A story is told about how the attendant of a Zen master of recent times was surprised to note that although he spread out the master's *futon* every night and placed a clean sheet over them, the sheet never became dirty. Later the attendant realized that the master was sleeping in the zazen position and so never used the *futon*. Another story tells us that the famous warlord Date Masamune (1566–1636), also made a habit of sleeping in the zazen position.

In present-day Zen monasteries, with the exception of *rohatsu dai sesshin,* the monks are allowed at the end of the day to remove their outer robes, unroll their *futon,* and sleep wrapped up in them, monks in Soto Zen monasteries sleeping on their right sides while those in Rinzai Zen monasteries sleep on their backs. In some monasteries monks are allowed to use their zazen cushions as pillows, while in others a part of the *futon* is rolled up and used for the same purpose. In still other monasteries the monks are not allowed to use any pillows at all and must place their heads directly on the wooden rail that runs along the edge of the raised platform on which they sleep. One hour after the sleeping period has begun, an official of the monastery makes an inspection. After that, those who wish to may quietly take their zazen cushions to a veranda of the monastery into the monastery gardens and continue their practice of zazen.

13 · Monks and Drinking

While it is true that monastic life involves various hardships, as one gradually accumulates experience, deepening his self-understanding and thereby gaining self-confidence, there are accompanying joys. After having become an experienced monk, a man is able to perform the required monastic activities nearly as well as the roshi. As one of the yearly monastic activities the monks hold a lively party on the evening preceding the winter solstice. Hoshu Miyajima-roshi has compared this party with that held by Christians on Christmas Eve. Making rice cakes at New Year's time, and eating the refreshments that are donated by pious laymen on special occasions throughout the year are also welcome respites in the monastic routine. Daisetz Suzuki has noted in his book, *The Training of the Zen Monk,* that the monks sometimes practice sumo (Japanese wrestling), but recently they have taken to playing baseball as well. Last but by no means least, it is no exaggeration to say that sake is inseparable from the life of Zen priests.

Gempo Yamamoto-roshi, for example, was one of those who liked sake, and it is said that he left instructions at his death to have the mourners at his funeral provided with ample quantities of it. It is true, however, that one of the ten major commandments of the Zen sect concerns alcohol. Gazan-roshi, head of the Tenryu-ji branch of the Rinzai Zen sect was, by nature, a person who liked to drink sake. When he was still a minor monastery official in training at Ibuka's Shogen-ji, he and some other monks became boisterous and started quarreling after having gotten secretly drunk in his room. The master, Tairyu-roshi, heard the commotion and thundered out, "Who's drinking in that monastery official's room?" Gazan answered with equal vociferousness, "If it's wrong to drink in a monastery official's room, how about the room of the head of this monastery?" Tairyu-roshi himself liked sake, but to restore order he had no other choice than to make a mutual pledge of abstention with Gazan and the other monks. He then gave an order that sake was not to be allowed in the monastery. This order had been in effect for more than a year when a lay devotee, feeling sorry for Tairyu-roshi, secretly sent him a bottle of *mirin* (a kind of sweet sake) to protect his health in his old age. Gazan discovered the *mirin* during the roshi's absence, and drank the greater part of it, pouring the remainder on the tatami. When the roshi returned Gazan pretended nothing had happened, but the roshi discovered the mischief anyway and thought, "This is undoubtably the work of Gazan and his fellow rascals!"

Not much later he rescinded his prohibition against sake. I think this exchange reveals something of the character of Zen priests.

There is a story according to which Tessen Yamaoka-osho boldly flung Emperor Meiji (reigned 1868–1912) down after having been ordered to be his opponent in a sumo match. According to the book *Tessen-koji no Shin Memmoku* (The True Character of Tessen) what actually happened is quite different. It seems that one evening, when Emperor Meiji was still a young man, he invited Tessen to have dinner with him and one of his chamberlains. During the course of the evening, while they were drinking, Emperor Meiji asserted, "From now on Japan, too, must become a country governed by law rather than decree." In response to this statement the emperor's chamberlain spoke of the necessity of morality as an important factor in ruling the nation. The emperor then asked Tessen what he thought about the matter, and Tessen replied that if Japan was to be ruled by laws alone, the people would eventually stop paying reverence at the shrine of the imperial family. This remark hit the emperor in a tender spot, and he was unable to reply. Instead, and because he had already had a great deal to drink, he got angry, and finally reached the point where he challenged Tessen to wrestle against him in a sumo match. Tessen believed it undesirable for a commoner to fight with the emperor, so he bowed deeply, and explained that he could not act as an opponent. The emperor became even more incensed by Tessen's refusal and he made a lunge at Tessen, trying to strike him in the eye with his fist. But Tessen moved his body in such a way that the emperor lunged past him, and the emperor fell down, injuring himself slightly and getting even angrier.

Later, after the emperor sobered up, Tessen admonished him severely and made him promise to abstain from both alcohol and sumo. Tessen then returned home, where he stayed for the next month in spite of frequent summonses from the emperor to attend this or that gathering. After a month elapsed, he suddenly accepted an invitation from the emperor and presented him with twelve bottles of grape wine. The emperor was extremely pleased with this gift and, thinking that it was now all right for him to drink, proceded to consume the wine in Tessen's presence. I think that in this story it is possible to see Tessen's resolute character, which he had developed through Zen and *kendo* (Japanese-style fencing), as well as his sympathetic consideration for others.

Tessen died at the age of fifty-three from cancer of the stomach, which is thought to have been caused to a great extent by heavy drinking. Koshu-osho, head of the Daitoku-ji branch of the Rinzai Zen sect for more than ten years during the middle of the Meiji era, died from the same cause when he was sixty-seven. He was extremely severe when giving guidance in Zen and often took part in doing monastic manual labor. He also had a taste for sake, and the story goes that after he had drunk a little, while away from the monastery, he would become a playmate for whatever children might be about, completely unaffected in his attitude.

According to Haku'un Yasutani-roshi, his master, Sogaku Harada-roshi, said, "If you like sake I won't say not to drink it, but you should efface yourself when drinking. With a realization of how difficult it is to escape from one's destiny, you should be careful not to lose your sense of shame or your feeling of repentance." Sake drinking is one of the appealing traits of Zen priests, but dying from stomach cancer as the result of excessive drinking is certainly not a distinction for a disciple of the Buddha.

Ekken Kaibara has written in his book *Yojokun* (Rules for Health Preservation), "Sake is the nectar of heaven. It is extremely beneficial because just a little will cheer you up, calm hot-headedness, improve the appetite, and cause sorrow to be replaced by pleasure." In a similar vein, Dr. Koji Kondo, has written about a talk he had with Daisetz Suzuki concerning the latter's diet. He asked whether he drank liquor or not, to which Suzuki replied that he drank a little. Dr. Kondo had expected Suzuki to say no and so was a bit amused at his answer. Suzuki then went on to remark that if taken in small amounts sake is a good thing, especially if it is savored.

One time I visited Suzuki at his home and in the course of the conversation I put the same question to him that Dr. Kondo had. His answer then was, "I eat and drink anything." To which his assistant added, "But he doesn't drink very much." By way of refutation Suzuki replied, "There are times when I do drink quite a lot."

14 · Searching for the Way

One of the characteristics of Zen training is that as their training deepens the *unsui* will make pilgrimages to visit various masters and monasteries. At first a monk chooses a master, under whom he should train determinedly until he masters the essentials of Zen. Following this, it is the general rule to deepen one's training by studying under various other masters, becoming familiar with their individual styles. It should be noted, however, that in reality this is not always the case.

The founder of the Chinese Rinzai Zen sect, Lin-chi, studied devotedly under Hsi-yun of the Obaku Zen sect for three years. When asked by a brother disciple whether or not he had ever asked Hsi-yun any questions concerning Buddhism during this time, he answered, "No, I haven't. What should I ask him?" "Ask him what the central point of Buddhism is," answered his brother disciple. When Lin-chi went and asked this question, instead of an answer Hsi-yun gave him a severe beating with a stick. After explaining what had happened to his brother disciple, he was told to go visit the master once more. Once again, however, he was struck when he asked the same question. Yet again his brother told him to go, and yet again he was struck. Finally, he became disheartened and because he thought there was no hope for him, he decided to leave the monastery. When he informed his brother disciple of his decision, he was told to notify Hsi-yun of his departure. Hsi-yun told him, "Go visit Ta-mo; he will certainly tell you something of value." Lin-chi went directly to Ta-mo's temple and there he was asked, "Where did you come from?" "I came from Hsi-yun's monastery," he answered. Being asked, then, what Hsi-yun had told him, Lin-chi explained how he had asked the same question three times and been beaten three times. He finished his account and asked, "Did I do something wrong?"

"Hsi-yun was so polite to you, and yet you ask such a foolish question as whether or not you did something wrong," thundered Tao-mo. At this Lin-chi realized enlightenment and said, "The teaching of Hsi-yun doesn't amount to much at all." This encounter marked the beginning of his extremely active dissemination of Zen.

Byakuin-zenji entered the Zen priesthood at the age of fifteen when he became a disciple of Tanryo-osho of Matsuin-ji. During a period of nine years he made pilgrimages to ten different temples. At the age of twenty-four, when he heard the temple bell of Eigan-ji (in Takada, Niigata Prefecture), he suddenly realized enlightenment. Soon after he visited Kei-tan Dokyo on Mount Han, overcame his self-conceit and, after training for a period of six months, was able to master the deepest secrets of Zen. Subsequently he returned to Shoin-ji, where as a result of devoting himself to severe post-enlightenment training, he damaged his lungs and began to suffer from dizziness and heartburn. After he was given up as a hopeless case by a doctor, he went to the Shirakawa region, east of Kyoto, where he visited a religious hermit by the name of Byakugen and received instruction from him concerning a method of meditative introspection. His subsequent miraculous recovery is recorded in the famous *Yasen Kanwa*. Byakuin was then recommended for the post of head priest of Shoin-ji, although he did not actually begin giving instruction there until nine years later, when he had completed pilgrimages to more than ten additional temples.

Gempo Yamamoto-roshi, who was called "the reincarnation of Byakuin," and who died five years ago at the age of ninety-six, was afflicted with an eye disease when he was about twenty-one years old. He was told by his doctor that he was going blind, and he then divorced his wife and made repeated pilgrimages to various temples on the island of Shikoku. On his seventh pilgrimage, at the age of twenty-four, he fell ill at Sekkei-ji (in Kochi). While he was recovering there, he met Taigen Yamamoto-roshi, and subsequently entered the Buddhist priesthood as his disciple. Later he trained for periods of two years each at Eigen-ji, Shofuku-ji, and Hofuku-ji. At Hofuku-ji he was struck with a bow by Kyuko-roshi, who had the reputation of being the severest master anywhere. He went next to Eiho-ji at the age of thirty-two, and there he studied under Dokutan-roshi. At that time there were always more than one hundred monks in training there, and Gempo-zenji is said to have been put in charge of the monastery kitchen for a long time. As a result of this training he was able to boast, "I am an expert cook. Although I'm not able to do anything else, I am proud to say that I have no equal anywhere when it comes to cooking."

Due to Taigen-roshi's illness, Gempo returned to Sekkei-ji at the age of thirty-seven; and after the roshi's death he attempted to reconstruct the temple. When he was forty-three he turned over Sekkei-ji to a friend and made a pilgrimage to Empuku-ji, where he trained earnestly both day and night for the next eight years under the guidance of Sohan-roshi. Finally he was given permission to carry on this roshi's line of teaching and became the head priest of Ryutaku-ji when he was fifty years old. Gempo lived to the ripe old age of ninety-six. His instruction in Zen, which put emphasis on breath control, made a great impact on those around him. A year or two before his death he is said to have instructed Kozo Ushida to "lengthen his breathing." He also told his successor, Soen Nakagawa-roshi, "I take about one breath every thirty minutes."

In Okina Takagi's book, *Gempo-roshi,* there is an anecdote concerning Gempo when he was in training at Empuku-ji, one part of which I would like to recount here. Gempo was acting as Sohan-roshi's attendant and also as a supervisor of the other *unsui.* Among the *unsui* he was highly respected and they addressed him as Inkyo-san (retired master), referring to the fact that he had retired from his former position as head priest of Sekkei-ji. His responsiblities as supervisor were not at all easy. It was he who would order the *unsui* to go to present their "answer" to the roshi concerning the *koan* he had given each of them to "solve." Since Gempo was required to give the order only five or ten minutes after they had gone there the first time, many of the *unsui* refused to go again, feeling, naturally, they had not had sufficient time to form a new opinion. Some *unsui* would even wrap both arms around a pillar in the Zendo and Gempo would be forced to whack their hands with a *keisaku,* the long wooden stick generally used to wake drowsy monks during zazen. At other times he would go behind the pillar-clinging monks and tell them. "All right, go!" and to pull them loose he'd give a sharp jerk on the cord that all Zen monks have tied around their waists. One day, a clever monk tied his waist cord so that it would come undone if it were pulled. When Gempo gave the monk's cord a hard jerk, he ended up falling flat on his back on the stone floor of the Zendo.

There were also some *unsui* who liked to smoke. One monk, who thought he wouldn't be noticed, was smoking behind the toilet when Gempo discovered him. The *unsui* was afraid of being scolded and bolted into the nearby mountains. He didn't attempt to return to the monastery until time for the evening meal, which as it turned out, was a special treat of mixed rice and vegetables. Unfortunately for this *unsui,* Gempo was still standing sternly with *keisaku* in hand waiting for him. This frightened the monk again, and he fled back into the mountains and so he missed out on the special evening meal. It wasn't until late that night that he was finally able to sneak back into the monastery. I've been told that in spite of Gempo's harsh methods, all of the monks who were subject to his severe discipline eventually became distinguished Zen priests.

I cannot help thinking that the making of pilgrimages as emphasized in Zen is an extremely fine training method, whether viewed from the perspective of the present age or of the whole world. In Germany a student is able to graduate even if he has spent as many as two years out of four at universities other than the one in which he originally enrolled. And in the United States many students do their postgraduate studies at a different university from the one in which they did their undergraduate work. The universities there not only hire teachers from among their own graduates but also gather men of talent from a wide field, preventing the sterility of self-fertilization. These practices indicate to me that the ancient training methods of Zen are far more rational than those presently in use at such Japanese colleges as Tokyo University. As has been noted on page 133, Shikyo-zenji, who reestablished monastic facilities at Empuku-ji, showed an amazing degree of rational thinking in his plan to open Empuku-ji's facilities to true Zen masters possessing moral influence and to earnest *unsui* from all over the country. Unfortunately, however, as people's desire for enlightenment has weakened, the rigor of monastic training has gradually disappeared, making it difficult for Zen, too, to save itself from falling victim to self-fertilization.

15 · Among the People: The Ten Oxherding Pictures

As the gardens and buildings of Zen temples, especially those having monastic facilities, are kept in good order, and the behavior of the monks is regulated so as to not admit any disturbance, the ordinary visitor is given the impression of a sacred area that is extremely difficult to approach. This order reflects good form, but the essence of Zen is to use form to go beyond form, to go beyond all discrimination and "let go of everything." The last of the familiar ancient *The Ten Oxherding Pictures,* which is entitled, *Entering the Marketplace with Helping Hands,* expresses this attitude very well. In describing this scene the twelfth-century Chinese Zen master Kuo-an states, "The gate of his [the enlightened man's] cottage is closed and even the wisest cannot find him. His illusory thinking has finally disappeared. He goes his own way, making no attempt to follow the steps of earlier masters. Carrying a gourd filled with wine, he strolls into the marketplace; leaning on his staff, he returns home. He leads innkeepers and fishmongers in the [Buddhist] Way."

"Entering the marketplace with helping hands" means to enter into the ordinary world of defilement and extend assistance to the masses. If a superior man lives in a wretched-looking hut no one is aware of how fine a person is present in their midst. At times such a person will go barechested and barefooted into the marketplace to buy wine or other goods, always smiling, showing absolutely no concern even if his face is dirty or mud clings to his clothing. When other people see his smiling face, they, too, can't stop smiling and they forget all their troubles. According to the poem by Kuo-an that accompanies this picture:

> Barechested, barefooted,
> He comes into the marketplace.
> Muddied and dust-covered,
> How broadly he grins!
> Without need of mystic powers,
> He swiftly brings
> Withered trees to bloom.

This is the same attitude Lao-tsu has expressed in his teaching, "Doing nothing, and yet leaving nothing undone," and in his concept of equality. But this attitude should not be confused with simple idleness. If it is necessary, the "helping hands" of such an enlightened person are not beyond wielding an iron bar to destroy resolutely and thoroughly all forms of illusion. In Shakko-zenji's commentary on this picture he writes, "Such a man, wielding an iron bar with incredible speed, is able to distinguish all and penetrate all."

Nanzen-ji's Shibayama Zenkei-roshi, has made a comparative study of the various commentaries that have been written about these pictures. In his book, *Ju Gyu no Zu* (The Ten Oxherding Pictures), he says that the true dwelling place of a Buddha, i.e., an enlightened person, lies beyond the realm of a saint, a place where, "being freed from discriminative thinking, his true Self can emerge." Furthermore, the conduct of a Buddha does not exist in some supramundane sphere; on the contrary, he lives in the quite ordinary world in such a way that "the wisest can detect about him no sign of perfection, his self having completely disappeared." Living his entire life in the natural world, it makes no difference to him what the circumstances he finds himself in may be. Leaving no traces of his passing, he continues to live in unity with himself and the universe. In the life of that rustic saint, Toku'un, who in the course of succeeding experiences finally achieved full enlightenment, we can see that seemingly miraculous power that "swiftly brings withered trees to bloom." Shibayama-roshi goes on to say that the refreshing nature of Zen-influenced painting, literature, and other arts is derived from the freedom that is expressed in this power which, in reality, is no power.

This state is also the ideal of Zen and a goal to which the Zenists' efforts should be directed. However, it is not something which can be easily or quickly achieved. *The Ten Oxherding Pictures* teach us that there are nine stages through which one must pass before arriving at the final goal. As each of these stages has been carefully explained in other books I would like to present only a brief explanation of each one.

In picture one, *Seeking the Ox,* the ox symbolizes the seeker's true Self, or "Buddha-nature." At this point he can only learn about this nature by going around and asking others. In picture two, *Finding the Tracks,* he is able to realize in which direction his goal lies. Picture three, *First Glimpse of the Ox,* describes the stage in which he first catches sight of the goal; but it is only a quick glance and the details are still unclear. He would be making a big mistake to think that what he had seen was the whole ox. Omori-roshi has said that if one's enlightenment did not go as far as *Catching the Ox,* which is picture four, it could not be said to be genuine. Even though the seeker has caught the ox, it is still unruly, and it is still necessary to use a whip for its domestication. In picture five, *Taming the Ox,* the ox has been thoroughly domesticated. Omori-roshi explains this by saying, "Frequenting the realm of discrimination [i.e., discriminative thinking] a man goes beyond all attachment [to things] by becoming one with the objective world. It is this tamed ox that represents the tempering of his selfless Self, and corresponds to post-enlightenment training." In picture six, *Riding the Ox Home,* the ox is no longer able to run away, the rider and the ridden becoming one. Picture seven is *Ox Forgotten, Self Alone.* Having searched for [and found] the ox, the seeker comes to realize that from the very beginning this ox was none other than oneself. Consequently, the ox disappears. Passing beyond the stage of *Ox Forgotten, Self Alone* he arrives at picture eight, *Both Ox and Self Forgotten,* in which even the holy position of a saint is denied. Or, as stated in *Sanzen Nyumon,* "Absolute negation, bereft of both subject and object, is provisionally represented in the form of a circle." In picture nine, *Returning to the Source,* the

seeker passes even beyond absolute nothingness until he returns to the real world of discrimination, realizing that mountains are indeed mountains and rivers are indeed rivers. Unless one bears discrimination in mind and conforms to it, it will be impossible to accomplish the primary vow sustaining Buddhist training, i.e., the vow to save all sentient beings. The subject matter of picture nine is, however, still limited to natural scenery; ordinary men and women do not appear as yet. Even priests who have studied Buddhism in the mountains for as long as twelve years must return again to the ordinary lay world if they are to complete their training.

It is for this reason that picture ten, *Entering the Marketplace with Helping Hands,* must be added. "Always joyful, he spent his whole life walking as a mendicant, living alone in the mountains and listening to the voice of nature. However, he would also visit the nearby villages, playing with the children and drinking wine with the farmers. When playing with children, he would even forget the passing of time; and when drinking wine, he would go to sleep on the dike between the ricefields. And if he met a poet, he would talk about poetry; and if he were asked to, he would read his own poetry. He wrote more than four hundred poems in the Chinese style and more than one

THE TEN OXHERDING PICTURES

1. Seeking the Ox

2. Finding the Tracks

3. First Glimpse of the Ox

4. Catching the Ox

5. Taming the Ox

6. Riding the Ox Home

7. Ox Forgotten, Self Alone

8. Both Ox and Self Forgotten

9. Returning to the Source

10. Entering the Marketplace with Helping Hands

thousand in Japanese style. His critics all agree that his poems express the elegance of lonely mountains, and echo with the reverberations of the *Man'yoshu* (Japan's oldest anthology of poems, c. 759). Likewise, people who have seen the poems in his own handwriting that have been preserved to the present day are unanimous in their praise of his skill as a calligrapher."

The preceding, which might well be called a description of a rustic saint, is the way in which Toyoji Togo, a noted scholar of Ryokan, introduces his readers to Ryokan-osho in the preface to his book by the same name. Ryokan was born in Izumozaki in Niigata Prefecture. At the age of twenty-two he met Tokusen of Entsu-ji (in Okayama Prefecture), when the latter was on a preaching tour. Shortly afterward he entered the Buddhist priesthood, became Tokusen's disciple, and went to Entsu-ji, where he trained for nearly twenty years. Then, with no apparent purpose in mind, he returned to his birthplace and for the next thirty years led a life like that described above.

Ryokan lived alone in a hermitage called

Gogo-an, and provided for his needs through mendicancy. He is recorded as having said, "The mission of people in religious orders is to devote themselves completely to the salvation of ordinary men and women. One should always be standing in the village streets, hands in the *gassho* position and bowing to the common people." At another time he said, "Not only the old farm people who braid straw while quietly waiting for their end but also the robust young men and women who work in the fields, and even the small children who play innocently in the woods by the village shrine, must become the objects of religious salvation."

At this point I would like to introduce three poems from Professor Togo's book on Ryokan. They are all concerned with how Ryokan loved to play with children. He has finished practicing mendicancy in the village streets and

1

He walks leisurely
Near the village shrine.
Spying him,
The children all shout:
"The funny priest
Has come again!"

2

Day after day after day,
He spends playing with children.
Two or three balls always in his sleeves,
Intoxicated by the balmy spring.

3

Hair unkempt, ears sticking out,
His tattered robes
Swirling like smoke,
He walks home—tipsy—
With hordes of children
Swarming all around.

It is generally accepted that the foremost worries of ordinary people concern poverty and sickness. If one more worry were added to these, it would probably concern human relationships. Awakening to one's true Self, thereby achieving fundamental peace, is the highest happiness there is. But for ordinary people the solution of their immediate problems takes first priority. It is no exaggeration to say that one of the strong points of Christianity, and the various so-called new religions of Japan (e.g., Soka Gakkai, Tenri-kyo, Rissho Kosei-kai) is that they devote a large part of their efforts to finding solutions to such problems. When Buddhism first came to Japan, Buddhist leaders like Prince Shotoku (reigned A.D. 593–623) devoted a great deal of attention to building hospitals and schools, and providing assistance for the poor and the aged. In the Kamakura period priests like Ninsho, head of Shitenno-ji, carried on this tradition. On the whole, however, although Buddhist practice and belief were purified through the emergence of new Buddhist sects, its social concern was considerably weakened. A notable exception to this decline was the Obaku Zen sect, which was active in social work. And individual Zen priests, such as Tetsugen-zenji, also carried on various social enterprises.

Tetsugen-zenji was originally a priest of the Jodo (Pure Land) sect who later converted to Obaku Zen, which he studied under Ingen and Mokuan. Later, he decided to print a new edition of the whole Buddhist canon, the Tripitaka, and to obtain funds he made a pilgrimage through the entire country collecting donations from as wide a range of persons as possible. A thousand *ryo* (a unit of old Japanese coinage) of platinum was given to him as a donation by one nun; and, in all, he was able to collect quite a sum of money. But just as he was to begin printing, a tidal wave struck the city of Osaka, producing a great number of refugees. Tetsugen then decided to use the money for relief measures for the disaster victims rather than for printing the Tripitaka. Later he once more set about collecting donations for his original project, and in 1681 he succeeded in raising enough money to have wooden printing blocks carved for all 6956 volumes of the Tripitaka. But, once again, disaster struck. From the winter of that year an extremely severe famine gripped the country, and in February 1683 he began to organize relief measures. At the end of the same month, he was taken ill, probably the result of having caught the plague, which was then quite prevalent. He died shortly thereafter on March 7, having sacrificed his life in helping the famine victims.

Zen is a religion which is inclined to be somewhat high-browed and ascetic. However, if one truly takes seriously the Bodhisattva vow to save others even at the expense of throwing away one's own peace, then one ought to become even more earnestly engrossed in compassionate practices as expressed by "entering the marketplace with helping hands." In this regard I think Zen could learn a great deal from the social-oriented activities of the Quakers.

16 · The Problem of Marriage

About ten years ago I met Alan Watts on one of his visits to Japan. During our discussion I asked why he believed that Japanese Zen in comparison with Chinese Zen is not true Zen. He replied that it was because Japanese priests get married. I then explained that although ordinary Zen priests do marry, the chief Zen masters, for the most part, remain unmarried. This is true even today. At the same time, even within the ranks of the highest Zen masters, there are some who are married, as are almost all ordinary priests. Because of this situation it is difficult to say what the true position of Zen priests is in regard to marriage. In China or Southeast Asia, on the other hand, a priest generally loses his status if he marries.

A Soto Zen head priest whose temple is located in the country and who is actively engaged in giving instruction in zazen, made the following lament about his celibacy: "I am not married and I have sent my disciples to school and looked after them in various ways. Recently, however, I seem to have become regarded as somewhat eccentric."

Even today Roman Catholic priests remain celibate, and until recently their celibacy was accepted as a matter of course. And the writer Tsutomu Minakami, who in his youth lived as a novice priest in a temple, has revealed the wretched life of obscurity that the common-law wife of a Zen priest was forced to live.

Many leading Zen figures of the past were married at one time or another. The seventeenth-century Zen master, Bunan-kokushi, for example, originally was the owner of an inn at Sekigahara and had both a wife and children. When he was more than forty years old, however, he left his family to enter the priesthood. Yamamoto-roshi divorced his wife before he entered the priesthood. Sugawara-roshi of Kencho-ji fell in love during the period he was in Zen training and eventually left the priesthood to get married. Soon after, however, he divorced his wife in order to resume his training. Thus, although it is true that many Zen masters in the past were married, it is also true that when they achieved the status of leaders none of them were bound by family encumbrances.

Sawaki-roshi has written in his autobiography, *Living in Zen,* that: "After I began my study [of Zen], I became so involved in it that I had no time to think about getting married.

In my case it wasn't a matter of trying hard to remain single, but simply that in endeavoring to go ahead in as straight a line as possible I have arrived at the present."

When one considers the necessity of Zen priests to make pilgrimages throughout the country to receive guidance from various Zen masters, it must be admitted that whether or not a man is burdened with family encumbrances can make a big difference. On the other hand, since in the course of having a family a man encounters much concrete human suffering it cannot be denied that such experience is useful in some respects in helping him to understand the life of ordinary people. I think that it is important that there be Zen masters who remain single, unbound by family encumbrances. Compared to married priests, such masters are far freer to devote themselves to their own training and the guidance of others. One step behind such masters there may be those priests who take a wife who is also interested in practicing Buddhism, bearing not more than two or three children. Having a helpful partner is often important in rendering assistance to others. Nevertheless, if one has many children they can become very great hindrances.

17 · The Problem of Education

For the objectives of Zen training to be realized in the larger society, it has long been held that various means must be used. In the widest sense of the problem all science and technology should be included as means. When one reflects seriously upon the first vow of the Bodhisattva—to save all sentient beings though their number be limitless—it is impossible not to regret that there is not a single Dr. Schweitzer to be found in present-day Japanese Zen or in Japanese Buddhism in general. This lack was vividly illustrated by the fact that when a Japanese medical assistance team was recently sent to Nepal, the area in which the Buddha was born, it was not sent by Japanese Buddhists but by Japanese Christians.

Another important problem is the kind of education future Zen leaders should receive. The seriousness of this problem is clearly seen in the fact that even famous Zen masters often make quite inaccurate comments on various social problems, losing a great deal of their credibility in the process. Various people, including Ryomin Akizuki, a present-day leading Zen master, are particularly worried about this problem. Although Zen priests do not need the knowledge of a scientist, there is still the necessity for them to have a sufficient understanding of the fundamentals of the social and natural sciences, philosophy, history, art, and the humanities in general, so that they will be able to make educated decisions. It is possible, of course, that a Zen master might wish to limit himself to simply giving guidance in Zen in the traditional manner; but in that case I think it would be advisable for him to remain silent in regard to social problems.

Another mistake which people engaged in Zen practice are prone to make is that since Zen makes "being in everything" its prime objective there is a dangerous tendency for present conditions simply to be accepted as they are. Such simple acceptance, however, could be more accurately described as the corruption of Zen rather than Zen itself. The true situation can be seen when one considers that it is Zen that stands in the wellspring of creativity and is in a process of daily renewal, and that it is Zen which boldly states that self-vigilance and self-awareness must never be neglected, emphasizing that Zen must be that which kills the Buddha and the Zen patriarchs and therefore kills even Zen when it is encountered.

In attempting to reform the present, however, it is also necessary to be aware of the law of causality, to be in love with destiny, and be ready to use present conditions as one's starting point. It is only then that one can use the power of natural laws to accomplish one's goals. The Zen life is something that has been polished by more than a thousand years of history, yet in its continual interchange with each new age it is something that must be ever emerging anew, creating itself in the process. Acquiring a broad foundation of learning is, I believe, necessary not only for Zen life in our present era but also for the realization of the Bodhisattva vow, "to save all sentient beings, though their number be limitless."

18 · For Life in a New Era

It has been more than ten years since the so-called Zen boom began in the United States.

Partially as a repercussion of this boom there has been a general increase in interest in Zen here in Japan, and the number of books written on Zen has increased like bamboo sprouts after a rain. When we consider this phenomenon we should realize that it is not simply a momentary fad and that we must strive to prevent it from becoming one.

In sharp contrast to this increased interest is the drastic decrease in the number of novice monks training at Zen monasteries, being only a shadow of what it was in the past. And while it is undeniable that traditional religions are growing progressively weaker in Japan, the new religions are flourishing as never before.

If Zen is simply the product of an earlier age that has lost its former value, then its decline is unavoidable. However, we modern followers of Zen believe that Zen is fully capable of including both religion and science and providing mankind with an unexcelled way of life. If this is so, then the question arises as to what kind of leadership as well as what type of life planning is necessary to develop Zen and make it meaningful to our new age. This is a question both for those Zen masters who are engaged in giving guidance to novice monks and those who are instructing laymen. In regard to the former group I do have a number of opinions, but since this is a question which requires an extremely detailed examination I would like to postpone a discussion of it at this time. Instead I would like to limit myself to a discussion of some new methods of Zen guidance for ordinary laymen, hoping that they may be of some help to my readers.

Ryomin Akizuki-roshi, in his book on *koan*, makes a distinction between the Zen transmitted from the historical Buddha (Tathagata Zen) and patriarchal Zen (Soshi Zen). Whereas Tathagata Zen arose in India, patriarchal Zen developed in China during the T'ang and Sung dynasties (A.D. 618–1279). He places particular emphasis on this latter form of Zen as well as the tradition which developed from it. From the psychological point of view I find it hard to agree with his rather arbitrary distinction, but in regard to his attempt to make Zen meaningful to our new age by presenting a new proposal, I feel as if we share the same mind. As the leader of a Zen group at Tokyo's Ochanomizu Women's University, the Kikusui-kai, Akizuki-roshi has had experience in giving instruction to women students, and he feels that there is a need for a place where laymen can study Zen and practice living apart from the normal Zen monastery where monks train. For this reason he is hoping for the construction of a student dormitory to be run on Zen principles.

In the suburbs of Kyoto is the Nagaoka

Zen Center run by Shonen Morimoto-roshi, a person for whom Akizuki-roshi has great respect. Akizuki-roshi's plans are not yet advanced to the point where he is ready to open such a center, but he is convinced that he would like to provide a place where "motionless" zazen could be united with the practice of more active Japanese arts such as the tea ceremony, poetry, the *koto,* the bamboo flute known as the *shakuhachi,* the chanting of traditional No plays, traditional dancing, and such Japanese martial arts as *kendo, karate,* and *aikido.* In the Kikusui-kai Zen group one of his female students followed his recommendation to practice *aikido* and did so at a gym until she graduated a year and a half later. At the time of her graduation she also received her black belt in *aikido;* and, according to the roshi, not only was her body firm but her eyes sparkled and she had become truly beautiful.

Akizuki-roshi has said that during work periods when he has heard his young girl students naturally join their voices in chorus, he has come to feel that the students need not limit themselves to reciting sutras to the accompaniment of the *mokugyo* drum, but they might also try to write hymnlike songs as well.

Another person who is engaged in giving training with unique features is Sogen Omori-roshi, the author of *Sanzen Nyumon,* which I have mentioned previously. In order to more completely understand his own spirit this roshi entered Tenryu-ji monastery where he devoted himself to Zen training, later combining the practice of Zen with Japanese fencing, in which he is an instructor. After having become the chief priest of Koho-in temple, which was founded by Tessen Yamaoka and is located in Tokyo's Nakano Ward, he has continued to give instruction in both Zen and fencing. Because of his broad vision and unassuming attitude he is one of the Zen masters living today for whom I have the highest respect. When Mr. Matsumura of Tankosha publishing company and I went to visit Omori-roshi one New Year's, we learned that the Chinese practice of *t'ai-chi* has many outstanding points as a martial art and that one of the forms of *aikido* could be made into a dance so women can master it more easily. Together with Zen and fencing, Omori-roshi was also giving instruction in calligraphy. He told us that after he has hung one of his student's calligraphy specimens on the wall of his room and looked at it for two or three days, he is able to discern the student's personality quite clearly.

Some time ago I received a small mimeographed pamphlet, on which were pasted many small photographs, from Akitsugu Wakamiya, a man who was a stranger to me at the time. In the accompanying letter he explained that the Creative Life Society (Seikatsu Sozo Kyokai), to which he belonged, had been helped in various ways by a book I had written, and that as a sign of the members' appreciation he was sending me the enclosed pamphlet which described their activities. To be frank, when I looked at the pamphlet I was quite surprised because many of the activities, no, even finer activities than I had previously thought of as the basis for a new type of Zen training, were actually being carried out in practice or were being attempted by his group. The day before I went to visit Omori-roshi, I visited Mr. Wakamiya's home where I had the opportunity to closely observe the group's daily activities with Mr. Matsumura, who accompanied me and recorded them on film.

Akitsugu Wakamiya's father was an earnest Christian who achieved fame as the head of the Matsumoto School for the Blind. The younger Mr. Wakamiya was also baptized as a Christian in his youth and received his religious education from his father. During his time at Waseda University, however, he became sick and was forced to drop out of school. After that, he became skeptical of Christianity and began studying Buddhism under Seika Goto and Gohei Ishimaru. He also lived for a time in one of Japan's new Buddhist-influenced religious communities, Ittoen, located in the suburbs of Kyoto. He studied psychoanalysis under Kenji Otsuki as well as the physiological health exercises of Harumichi Hida under his disciple and collaborator, Kurakichi Hiratauchi. About fifteen years ago he moved from Matsumoto to Tokyo where he became ill with asthma, suffered from poverty, and at one time even contemplated committing suicide. Finally as a result of a letter to the reader's column of a local newspaper in which he proposed "to establish a group which would make life worth living," a few people gathered around him and helped him to buy a house in Nakano Ward. He invited people with various spiritual problems to live together as one large family community, training both their minds and their bodies while seeking to create a new life.

The Creative Life Society's day begins at 5:45 A.M. with the sounding of wooden clappers and it encompasses a day full of various activities that lasts until past 10 P.M. After waking up, the members' immediate activities include a rub-down with cold water, cleaning both inside and outside their quarters, Japanese fencing practice with a wooden sword, yoga exercises, zazen, reciting sutras, and eating breakfast. Following breakfast those who must leave for work do so, while those who have time go out shopping for provisions, do their washing, or chop firewood. The two meals a day that are prepared for the whole group consist of unpolished rice mixed with wheat. In addition to this, various kinds of vegetables are liquefied in a juicer and drunk. Another dish in which this group takes pride, in addition to its Japanese pickles and bean paste soup, consists of large cabbage leaves on which they spread soybean paste specially brought from Japan's Shinshu District.

In the evening, after bathing with both hot and cold water, they conduct pronunciation exercises, and, depending on the day, choral singing, lectures, discussions, and sutra recitation practice. Kurakichi Hiratauchi visits the group to give medical treatments, using moxabustion and other techniques, and, on occasion, will provide guidance for fasting over a period of one to three weeks. Mr. Hiratauchi's guidance is very severe and, at times, he will revile the participants or even slap them on the cheek. One high school girl who thought that he wouldn't dare strike her, was dozing when she shouldn't have been and had her face slapped three or four times to wake her up. Sometimes he strikes the participants so hard that they are sent flying, and he has

even been known to have thrown them in a nearby pond. Although there was one woman university student who ran away while undergoing this kind of treatment, many others have had neuroses or asthma cured as a result of the same treatment. And in one case the head of a large city hospital, who was suffering from insomnia, asked to undergo this treatment.

The thing that has deeply impressed me about the Creative Life Society is that they have gathered together so many different good practices. In a university situation it would be very difficult to do this. That it has been able to be done at all is because Mr. Wakamiya himself was deeply troubled by problems concerning religious belief, the meaning of life, and his own health. It was only after he visited various teachers in search of solutions to his problems that he was able to initiate and give guidance in this new way of life. Receiving only enough money from the group's participants to cover actual costs he is continually taking care of approximately ten people. It is certain that without the infinite compassion of a Bodhisattva he would not be able to do this kind of work.

Guiding the group is not merely the work of Mr. Wakamiya alone; his whole family is involved. Although his wife is kept very busy with cooking and other household tasks, she also participates in Yoga exercises, zazen, and choral singing. Their two sons, one who is in junior high school and the other in senior high, also share the same room as the other participants and take part in the same activities when they are not occupied with their school work. It might well be said that the program run by Mr. Wakamiya is an expression of infinite compassion on the part of his whole family.

In the vast majority of the approximately 20,000 Zen temples in Japan it is safe to say that the head priest is married and living together with his family. But when one thinks that in only a few of them zazen is practiced by an entire family, it is hard not to be deeply moved by the example that Mr. Wakamiya and his family have set. Of course, the rules which his group follows are not yet as refined as those in a Zen monastery, but it would be no exaggeration to say that Zen is living in a very creative way thanks to his endeavors.

Dr. Bernard Phillips once said he had noted that in some Japanese Zen monasteries the monks were very slothful in their practice of zazen, though those in Hosshin-ji monastery seemed to be extremely earnest. I would say that the zazen of the Creative Life Society is similar to that of Hosshin-ji.

An important problem for all of us who are interested in Zen's future is the form and content of the guidance that should be given to those laymen whose interest in Zen has gradually increased of late.

19 · Zen: Fountainhead of Love and Creativity

As a measure of his high respect for Zen, the French psychoanalyst Hubert Benoit has called his book on Zen *Supreme Doctrine*. After forty years of acquaintance with Zen, with particular emphasis given in recent years to scientific research on the subject, I have come to feel that Zen embraces not only religion but science as well. As such it may well be the highest way of life in the world.

Erich Fromm, who studied Zen under the guidance of Daisetz Suzuki and founded a new school of psychoanalysis, placed particular emphasis in *Zen Buddhism and Psychoanalysis* (which he coauthored with Suzuki and

De Martino) on Suzuki's description of Zen as a method for awakening to our Original-nature, becoming free from various restrictions, being able to freely use the creative and compassionate impulses with which our spirits are endowed, and in this way finding happiness as a result of having been able to discover our inner potential for mutual love.

In the preface of *Toyo no Kokoro* (The Spirit of the Orient), which he wrote not long before his death in 1966, Suzuki has written: "Zen is that which penetrates to the limitless creativity at the bottom of our spirits." He then went on to say that we should act according to this creativity, emphasizing this positive aspect of Zen rather than its negative aspect that "all is relative."

From the standpoint of a psychologist I would like to point out the following characteristics of Zen. First, Zen is that which puts not only our life and body in order but our spirit and Self as well. Furthermore, because of a deep experience of the essential unity of our Self and the universe, we awake to our true-Self, thus being willing to work on behalf of all creation as a result of the deep love that spontaneously springs forth. I think that what Dr. Suzuki has described as limitless creativity is that which pours forth from our Original-nature after it has been tapped.

Postscript

In the middle of October several years ago, Yoshiichi Matsumura of Tankosha publishing company visited me. He told me that his company had had photographs taken over the past several years of the monastic life and annual religious events of Empuku-ji, and he asked if I would write my impressions of monastic life from the standpoint of a scientist, to be used with the photographs. As I had enjoyed a number of Tankosha's books, I felt I could not easily refuse his request.

I believe that within the essence of Zen there is that which is unexcelled in the world and that a new form of Zen is desirable to meet the needs of the new age. I also felt that if I wrote about Zen attitudes and life from this point of view, it would be possible to create something that would be valuable, to some extent at least, to people in general, and so I agreed to his request. Before this meeting I had written two books on Zen, *Shinri Zen* (Psychological Zen) and *Zen no Susume* (A Recommendation for Zen), and had been quite surprised at the extent to which they were read by the general public. I felt, however, that a description of actual Zen life would be an important supplement to my previous works. As it turned out,

I also learned a great deal in the process of writing the text.

For editorial and research assistance I am grateful to Mr. Shiro Usui, head of the editorial department of Tankosha, and his assistants. This book might be said to be the fruit of their active support. Tankosha's Mr. Matsumura was also kind enough to assist me in interviewing Akitsugu Wakamiya and Sogen Omori-roshi.

I am very much indebted for the kind assistance rendered me by Sokaku Toriyama-roshi and Genji Nakajima-roshi of Empuku-ji. For information concerning life at Rinzai Zen monasteries, I am indebted to Mumon Yamada-roshi, head of Kyoto's Hanazono University, Joku Kimura and Eshin Nishimura of the Zen Culture Research Institute, Shonen Morimoto-roshi of the Nagaoka Zen Center, and Soen Nakagawa-roshi of Ryutaku-ji. For detailed explanations of monastic rules and regulations I am indebted to Kakunen Ninshi Kataoka, a layman associated with Sokoku-ji as well as all the monks of that monastery. For information concerning unusual aspects of Soto Zen I was fortunate enough to receive an introduction from the head priest of Kyoto's Shusen-ji to Kakumyo Tsuji-roshi of Chigen-ji (in Miyazu). Thanks to Zenkei Shibayama of Nanzen-ji I was able to make copies of the valuable *The Ten Oxherding Pictures,* and it was Dr. Shunichi Okamoto, who lives near Okayama's Sogen-ji, who kindly sent me a collection of anecdotes concerning Tekisui-zenji and Gazan-zenji. In addition to the preceding I am also indebted to Tokan Hirazawa, Sogen Omori-roshi, Professor Toyoji Togo, Ryomin Akizuki, and the many others from whose writings I borrowed quotations. To all of these people I wish to express my deepest appreciation.

As I often do research in my seminar room at the university, I quite frequently receive the generous assistance of my associates there. This time was no exception, and I am indebted to Kozaburo Usui for having gone to the Obaku Zen sect's Mampuku-ji (in Uji, Kyoto) to find the answer to a question I posed concerning vegetarian food. In addition, Torao Maruyama was kind enough to read the manuscript. Both of these persons have been closely associated with Zen for quite some time, and I am grateful that our common interest in Zen has enabled us to unite our efforts in this way.

One deep regret I have is that the former head of the Gokoku-ji branch of the Rinzai Zen sect, Daiko Muishitsu Yamazaki-roshi, who had given me instruction in Zen since I was a student over forty years ago, died before this book was completed. I can still vividly remember the gentle look on his face and how happy he was to see me when I went to visit him at New Year's. When I began practicing zazen while still a student, I was overawed by his dignity. In later years I fondly remember how this dignity was combined with his serene countenance, the result of accumulated virtue. His acquaintanceship with such leading scholars as Dr. Shigenao Konishi, Dr. Momoe Miura, and others, as well as his training of such excellent laymen as Dr. Keiji Nishitani, professors Ninshi Kataoka and Jisuke Shikano, etc., can be said to be a result of such virtue. The Soto Zen sect in recent years has also seen the passing away one after another of such eminent masters as Horyu Ishiguro-roshi, Eko Hashimoto-roshi, and Kodo Sazaki-roshi. Fortunately I had various opportunities to deepen my understanding of Zen through contacts with these men, and this is all the more reason I realize how precious they were. I would like to humbly acknowledge once again the profound debt I owe to the kindness of these various roshi.

The "weathermark" identifies this book as having been planned, designed and produced at the Tokyo offices of John Weatherhill, Inc. Book design and typography by Ronald V. Bell. Layout of photographs by Tankosha, Kyoto. Gravure platemaking by Dai Nippon Printing Co., Tokyo. Gravure printing by Kinmei Printing Co., Tokyo. Composition and letterpress printing by General Printing Co., Yokohama. Bound at the Makoto Bindery, Tokyo. The text is set in 10-point Monotype Times New Roman with hand-set Lydian for display.